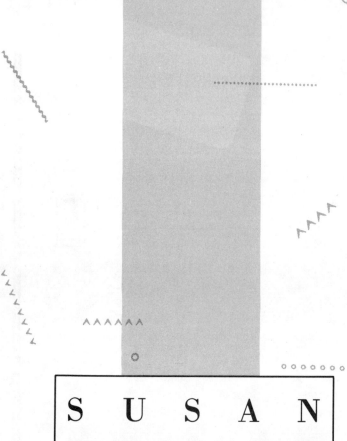

S U S A N
KESSLER

∘∘∘

A FIRESIDE BOOK

PUBLISHED BY SIMON & SCHUSTER INC.

NEW YORK LONDON TORONTO SYDNEY TOKYO

THE New Woman

FAST

~ AND ~

FABULOUS

MENU COOKBOOK

A FIRESIDE BOOK
Published by Simon & Schuster Inc.
Simon & Schuster Building
Rockefeller Center
1230 Avenue of the Americas
New York, NY 10020
FIRESIDE and colophon are registered
trademarks of Simon & Schuster Inc.

Designed by Bonni Leon

Manufactured in the United States
of America

10 9 8 7 6 5 4 3 2

Library of Congress Cataloging in
Publication Data
Kessler, Susan.
  The New woman fast and fabulous menu cookbook.

  "A Fireside book."
  Includes index.
  1. Cookery. 2. Menus. I. New woman.   II. Title.
TX652.K432 1988   641.5′52   88-3088
ISBN 0-671-64544-7

Some of these recipes have been previously
published in *New Woman* magazine.

To

LARRY ▲▲▲▲

for
encouraging
me and being
my best
friend

MY MOTHER ○○○○

for
instilling
in me a
certain
style of
entertaining

MY FATHER ＼＼＼＼

for
showing
me how to
have a
good time!

TABLE OF CONTENTS

ACKNOWLEDGMENTS

*O*ne of the nicest things about an acknowledgment page is that it gives me the opportunity to say a big thank you publicly to all those who have helped me find the right path and stay on it, and who have contributed their thoughts, tips, and recipes.

Six years ago I never would have dreamed of writing a cookbook. Actually, I never would have imagined writing anything at all, and that includes being the Food Editor of a major national magazine!

So thanks to . . .

My parents, whose entertaining skills rubbed off on me early and who gave me a good sense of how to help people have a good time.

My husband Larry, who always encouraged me to set higher goals for myself. He transformed a very shy and quiet seventeen-year-old girl from Michigan into an outgoing woman who can talk to anyone about anything and thinks she can accomplish whatever she sets her mind to. This book is my ultimate accomplishment, and without Larry's help and understanding, I probably wouldn't have attempted it. Also, he deserves a special thank you for tasting and critiquing many recipes that didn't quite follow his own dietary guidelines—and he didn't even complain too often!

Pat Miller, the Editor/Publisher of New Woman, who has given me the opportunity to do more and constantly challenged me to do it better.

Special thanks to Caroline Bowyer, Gordon Reynolds and Josh McHugh in the art and photo departments at New Woman who are responsible for the beautiful photographs appearing in this book. Also, thank you to photographers Rita Maas, Michael Skott, Michael Geiger, Steven Mark Needham, Constance Hansen, and Tom Eckerle.

Harvey Klinger, my agent, who made my New Year's Eve 1987 one of the best ever with one telephone call telling me he found a publisher for my cookbook.

My friends who responded to a questionnaire I mailed out asking them to share with me any of their own quick tips and recipes: Joni Muskovitz, Ellen Agress, Barbara Buchholz, Edward Moore, Zuzu Schatz, Nancy Druckman, Marilyn Krantz, Estelle Ballinger, Sally Figdor, Roberta Kaye, Dale Winston, Harry Agress, Judy Tenney, Elsie Wachtell, Lew Paper, Barbara Schlein, Pam and Howard Abrahams *(for their humorous response), Jane Mitchell (whose recipes go way back), Lee Kessler (my mother-in-law), Elissa Grossman (my sister), and Laura Zolkower (my mother).*

The biggest thank you goes to Janice Burne, who has shared numerous tips and recipes with me over the past fifteen years. She is an expert at developing recipes and has won many recipe contests. In addition to all that, she is a wonderful hostess and writer herself.

Julia Child, whose TV show in Boston taught me how to cook during the first year of my marriage.

My editor, Barbara Gess, who has put up with my constantly asking "Do you really think it's good?" and for letting me feel involved every step of the way. Also to everyone else at Simon & Schuster who has had a hand in giving my book its "good looks."

S.K.

NOTE ON RECIPES:

The menus for entertaining can be mixed and matched to include suggested accompaniments from the everyday menus. Some recipes in both sections might take a long time to cook, but I think of them as being quick because they require short preparation time. Many of the dishes can be prepared ahead (some can be frozen) and reheated without comprising quality, and others can be partly assembled, ready to be tossed together when needed.

INTRODUCTION

You might expect me to start off by saying I have been cooking since I was five years old and always dreamed about being a caterer and food writer. Actually, the truth is that my mother and grandmothers were wonderful cooks, especially bakers, and the only thing I ever did was help my mother decorate canapés with a pastry bag for parties that my parents would host. My mother used to call me the "Mix Queen" because I never knew how to make anything from scratch. When I met my husband, he taught me how to make hamburgers and tuna fish to survive! Well, I think I have come quite a long way since then.

Once we decided to stop eating red meat, I felt it was time to learn to cook properly if I was ever going to enjoy eating fish, among other things. We lived in Boston shortly after getting married and Julia Child's show on television taught me how to cook. I started buying cookbooks and reading them like textbooks. Before long, I was hooked. I used to spend days preparing elaborate food for fancy dinner parties and creating the perfect setting to go along with it. The setting is at least as important as the food.

I remember a Hawaiian luau party my parents gave, complete with a store mannequin wearing a grass skirt greeting guests on the front porch. The furniture was moved out of the dining room, a fountain was erected there complete with circulating water, synthetic grass was laid on the floor, and low dining tables were set up with guests sitting on the floor for dinner. Now that's a setting! Some of that zest for entertaining must have rubbed off on me.

In 1979 I started a catering business called Unforgettable Edibles. After all, I loved to cook, so why not get paid for it? More women were working and looking for a helping hand in the kitchen. My business thrived through word of mouth and was helped along by an article in *House and Garden* magazine in 1980. In 1982 I joined *New Woman* as food editor and in 1985, I suggested the idea of "Short Order Cook" to Pat Miller, *New Woman*'s editor/publisher. A caterer helps out the busy woman who wants to entertain. But what about the busy woman who needs to get dinner on the table for herself, her husband, and her children at the end of the day? A "Short Order Cook" column that would provide a recipe for an elegant main course that serves two and could be prepared in under thirty minutes was the perfect answer.

The column's recipes take advantage of short order cooking, which is based on a few simple techniques: steaming, grilling, broiling, sautéing, roasting, microwaving, and, easiest of all, buying take-out! This book extends the short order concept, and in addition to quick recipes, you will find relevant tips and useful information within each menu. I hope this will encourage you to curl up and read this like a textbook—better yet, a workbook.

In addition to the everyday main course recipes, a menu is suggested that is composed of simple go-withs and desserts you can cook without recipes (such as rice) or can be picked up at your favorite local gourmet shop (such as blueberry pie). Bear in mind, that the everyday main courses for two are special enough to be doubled or tripled for company. Don't be afraid to let yourself mix and match between the everyday and company menus. After all, you owe it to yourself after a hard day to sit down to a lovely dinner good enough for your most favored guest!

In addition to the nearly fifty Everyday Menus, the book goes ten steps further than the column and includes over thirty complete menus for entertaining. Each menu in the Entertaining section provides all the recipes needed to cook a complete dinner for six. There are numerous tips and entertaining thoughts and ideas for the perfect party that are meant to help get you out of the kitchen in no time without sacrificing quality. To save even more time, you might want to substitute some store-bought foods for some recipes in the menu. These company recipes may take more time than thirty minutes to cook in the oven, but the actual preparation time is relatively short.

Both the everyday and company menus include a beverage. The wine selections are broken down into categories, such as light, fruity red; medium-bodied, dry white, and so on. You will find a wine guide in the Appendix which lists some of my favorites in each category. It will help point you in the right direction when you go to the liquor store.

One of the most important things for the short order cook is to have a well-stocked pantry (see Chapter 1). If you have the basics on hand, you should just have to stop at the market for a few fresh items.

In addition to cooking dinner, try to make the time to set a pretty table even during the week. My husband and I have found the evening meal is the one we linger over the longest, sharing the events of the day. So, set the table, light the candles, open the wine, and begin to cook the short order way. *Bon appétit!*

CHAPTER 1

FAST AND FABULOUS COOK'S PANTRY

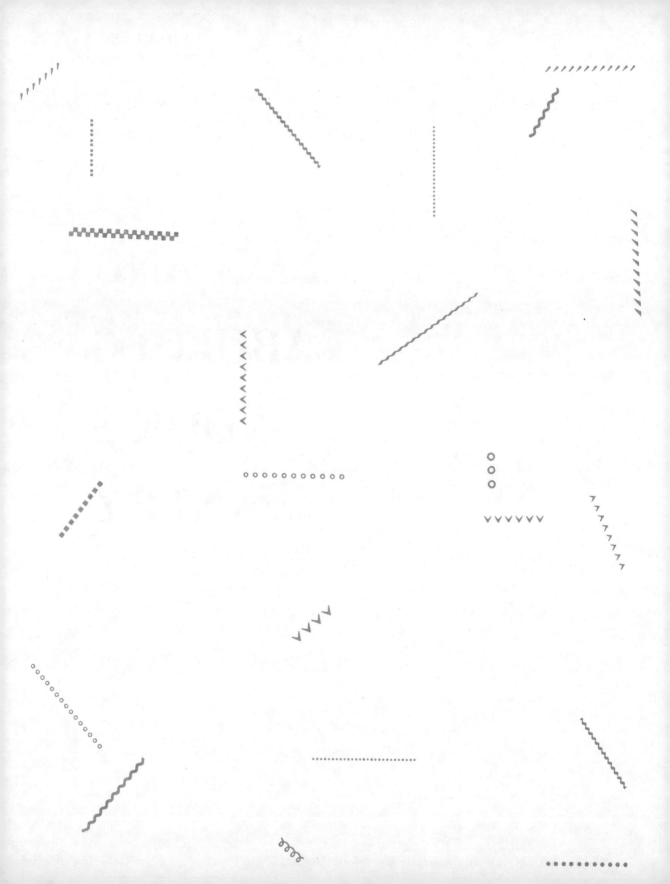

*T*he best short order cook is one who has a well-stocked kitchen. Grocery shopping for dinner can take up more time than the actual cooking does, so it pays to be prepared! In other words, take full advantage of your pantry, refrigerator, and freezer so that you are prepared (and stocked) for almost anything. With enough basics and gourmet treats, you can cook for yourself, your family, or company without much advance planning or even a trip to the supermarket.

For instance, if you have corn tortillas in the freezer, jalapeño peppers in the pantry, and cheddar cheese in the refrigerator, you have the makings of a hot Mexican open-face sandwich or hors d'oeuvre. With dried mushrooms in the pantry and eggs in the refrigerator, you have a wonderful wild mushroom omelette. For dessert, you can make a fabulous fruit tart with a prepared pastry crust and bottled lemon curd, and then decorate it with lemon slices and whipped cream or crème fraîche.

The list that follows is rather extensive and you would need a pantry the size of a gourmet shop to hold every item. These suggestions are meant to be just that—you can choose the assortment that appeals to your taste, needs, and style of cooking.

~~~PANTRY LIST

COOKING STAPLES

- *Assorted oils* olive, sesame, safflower, peanut, and corn
- *Assorted vinegars* red wine, white wine, rice wine, balsamic, sherry, and raspberry
- *Starches* spaghetti, angel hair, linguini, orzo, instant polenta, bulgur, couscous, white rice, brown rice, wild rice, Arborio, and kidney beans
- *Soups and stocks* chicken stock, beef stock, clam juice, cream of mushroom soup, and cream of shrimp soup
- *Herbs and spices* fresh herbs whenever possible, or dried—curry powder, herbes de Provence, paprika, saffron, cinnamon, cinnamon sticks, ginger, cayenne pepper, chili powder, red pepper flakes, bay leaves, cumin, nutmeg, cloves, sage, rosemary, thyme, basil, oregano, peppercorns, and tarragon

CANNED STAPLES

- red salmon caviar, baby shrimp, clams, salmon, tuna, and white meat of chicken (for easy chicken pot pie)
- anchovies and anchovy paste
- baby corn, roasted peppers, olives, artichoke hearts, sun-dried tomatoes (for hors d'oeuvres), and dried wild mushrooms (for omelettes)
- tomato paste, plum tomatoes, and tomato sauce
- nori (sheets of toasted seaweed)
- soy sauce, teriyaki sauce, salsa, Tabasco, Worcestershire, and hot pepper sauce
- lemon curd, preserves, jams, jellies, and chutneys (for glazes and omelette fillings)
- water chestnuts, capers, and jalapeño peppers
- crackers and melba rounds
- assorted mustards (Dijon, dry mustard, etc.)
- ice cream toppings

BAKING STAPLES

- semisweet and unsweetened chocolate squares, semisweet chocolate morsels, and cocoa
- unbleached flour, oatmeal, and cornmeal
- white sugar, brown sugar, confectioners' sugar, honey, and molasses
- vanilla, almond, and lemon extracts
- baking soda and baking powder
- assorted dried fruits (to use in fruit compote)

REFRIGERATOR LIST ~~~

- milk, sour cream, crème fraîche (keeps longer than heavy cream and good for use in sauces), and yogurt (the perfect buttermilk substitute)
- eggs
- mayonnaise
- bottled horseradish
- butter
- cheeses: Parmesan, Gruyère, Swiss, goat cheese, Roquefort
- lemons and limes
- oranges
- parsley
- potatoes
- onions
- dry yeast and fast-rising yeast

FREEZER LIST

- puff pastry, puff pastry shells, pastry dough, pizza or bread dough, and bread crumbs
- breads, rolls, and tortillas
- ice cream and sorbets
- frozen raspberries, strawberries, cranberries, and mashed bananas (for desserts)
- walnuts, almonds, and pecans (they stay fresh longer in the freezer)
- tortellini and ravioli
- homemade spaghetti sauce and pesto

WINE AND LIQUOR LIST (for cooking)

- white wine, red wine, vermouth, Madeira, Marsala, port, dry sherry
- bourbon, tequila, vodka, gin, light and dark rum
- Grand Marnier, brandy, applejack or Calvados, crème de cassis, kirsch, Sambuca
- beer

CHAPTER 2

TRICKS
OF THE
TRADE

When I was putting the finishing touches on this cookbook, I found there were more tips for each menu than there was room for. I didn't want to leave them out, so this chapter is made up of all sorts of tips that, for lack of a better way to put it, didn't quite fit anywhere else!

ALL ABOUT GADGETS

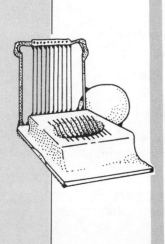

1. Use an egg slicer to slice mushrooms, after removing stems.
2. Use the pointed end of a pocket-type can opener to pry open oysters.
3. Use unwaxed dental floss to split cake layers and truss a chicken.
4. Use tweezers to remove bones from fish.
5. Sharpen scissors by cutting sandpaper.
6. When storing coated nonstick pans one inside the other, place paper plates between them to prevent scratching.
7. If you live in a humid climate, add a few grains of uncooked white rice to your salt shaker to keep it from clogging.

CUT DOWN MINUTES, DON'T CUT OUT BAKING!

1. Keep a sponge or paintbrush in a tub of margarine to use for greasing baking pans.
2. Preheat the oven as soon as you enter the kitchen.
3. If you have the room, keep your food processor and electric mixer assembled and ready to use.
4. Toasting nuts in a 350° oven for 5 minutes further enhances their flavor.
5. Keep a supply of nuts in the freezer at all times, stored in labeled, airtight plastic bags or freezer jars.
6. To soften butter quickly, microwave on HIGH for 7 to 10 seconds.
7. To reduce cleanup use paper baking cups when making muffins or cupcakes.
8. Chocolate morsels melt faster than chocolate squares.
9. Use fast-rising yeast and frozen piecrusts when appropriate.
10. Use an ice cream scoop to fill muffin and cupcake pans.
11. Use a large salt shaker filled with flour for dusting cake pans and work surfaces.
12. Use the divider from an aluminum ice cube tray to cut biscuits in a hurry. Roll out the dough, place on a cookie sheet, and cut with the divider, but don't separate. After baking pull apart.
13. Hard, cold butter will soften quickly if you first shred it and then let it stand for a minute.
14. Use a coarse grater to grate cold butter over pies to be dotted with butter.
15. When chopping dried fruits, spray your knife with nonstick vegetable shortening spray so the fruit won't stick.

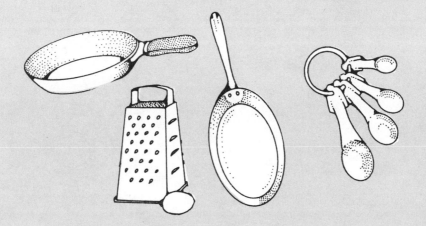

ALL ABOUT CLEANUP

1. Avoid the drudgery of defrosting your refrigerator by unplugging it for an hour once a week to avoid ice buildup.

2. Next time you accidentally drop an egg on the kitchen floor, sprinkle a layer of salt on it and let sit for a few minutes. It hardens the egg and makes cleanup a breeze.

3. To prevent sticking, rinse a saucepan with cold water before heating milk in it.

4. Before measuring anything sticky (i.e., molasses), coat a measuring cup with oil.

5. Use warm water when washing dishes soiled with egg.

6. To remove spots from copper-bottomed cookware, use a sponge and make a paste mixture of salt and white vinegar.

7. Remove residue left from sticky labels with nail polish remover, vegetable oil, or lighter fluid. Make sure to wash well afterward with soapy water.

THE FAST AND FABULOUS COOK'S STRATEGY TO GREAT FAST MEALS ⟩⟩⟩⟩⟩⟩⟩⟩⟩⟩⟩⟩

1. Eliminate pots and pans; cook and bake foods in disposable foil wrappers whenever possible.
2. Cook a big pot of soup or bake a large pan of lasagne. Reheat as needed in the microwave.
3. Start two meals at once by cooking enough pasta, rice, or potatoes for more than one dish.
4. Let the butcher do some work by slicing meat for stir-fry, cubing meat for stews, and boning cutlets.
5. Visit the salad bar in your supermarket for prepared vegetables to use in salads, stir-fry, casseroles, and vegetable dishes.
6. Buy an already-roasted chicken, cooked meats from the deli, or ready-to-heat entrées from specialty food shops.

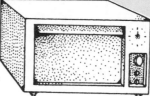

 ICROWAVE TIPS ∧∧∧ ∧∧∧∧∧∧∧∧∧∧∧

1. Heat liqueurs for flambéing on HIGH for fifteen seconds per ounce.

2. Reheat waffles and pancakes for quick breakfasts.

3. Soften a 1-quart carton of ice cream in the microwave on DEFROST for 30 to 40 seconds.

4. Plump raisins in water or liquor called for in a recipe by microwaving, covered, on HIGH for 3 minutes. Let stand for 3 minutes, drain well, and use.

5. Freeze leftover rice in 1- or 2-cup containers. Defrost and heat in one step in a covered bowl. Heat on HIGH for 2 to 3 minutes for 1 cup and 3 to 5 minutes for 2 cups, stirring twice.

6. Hasten ripening of an avocado by heating on MEDIUM for 2 minutes. Turn over and heat for 1 minute longer.

7. Cut grilling time by as much as half by partially cooking chicken in the microwave oven while coals heat.

8. Soften cream cheese by removing the foil wrapper and placing the cheese on plastic wrap. Heat on HIGH for about 15 seconds.

9. If a jar of honey has crystallized, remove the lid and heat on HIGH for less than a minute, then stir.

10. Acorn and other winter squashes can be difficult to cut. Heat on HIGH for 1 to 2 minutes to soften slightly.

11. After-dinner brandy can be heated on HIGH until warm, about 10 seconds.

12. To soften butter for easier spreading, put a stick of butter on a serving plate and heat on MEDIUM LOW (30 percent) for 10 to 15 seconds.

13. Tomatoes can easily be peeled by heating on HIGH for 15 seconds. Let stand for 1 minute and then peel.

14. Place 16 chocolate mint patties on a baked cake layer and heat on MEDIUM HIGH for 2 minutes for quick frosting. Remove and spread evenly.

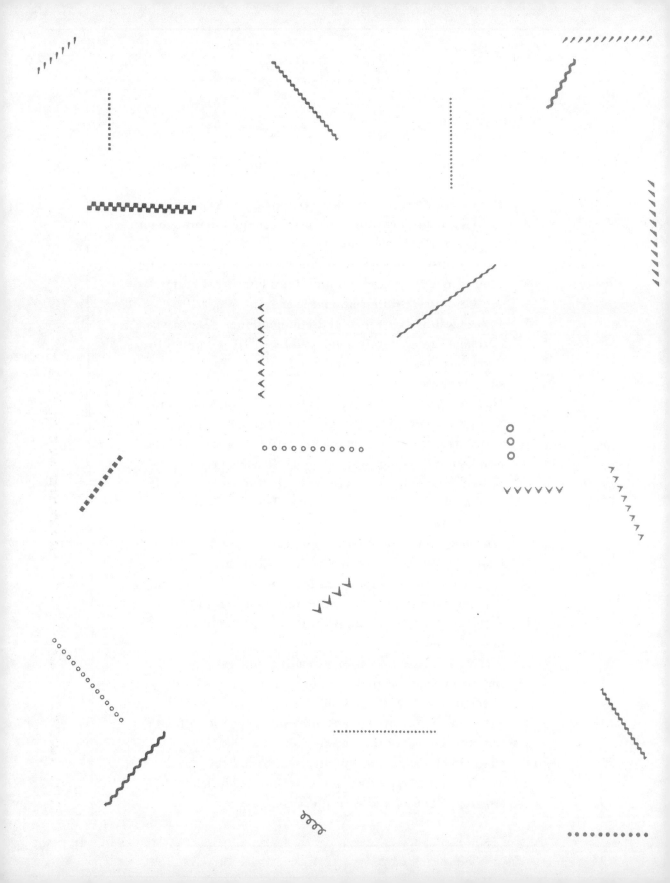

CHAPTER 3

EVERYDAY MENUS

FISH

QUICKEST DINNER OF ALL

MENU

ONE-MINUTE SALMON

SAUTÉED CUCUMBERS

STRAWBERRY BISCUIT CAKES

BEVERAGE: DRY, LIGHT-BODIED WHITE WINE

This fish cooks so quickly it is best to cook it directly on heatproof dinner plates. I paid $2.00 each for mine and they were well worth it. Prepare the cucumbers by cutting them into 1½-inch sticks. Sauté in a skillet with 1 tablespoon butter, salt, pepper, and chopped dill. Cook for about 2 minutes while the salmon is in the oven. Since this menu is so low-calorie and healthy you will have some room left to splurge on dessert. Slice the strawberries and set *aside to marinate in a bowl with a little sugar and kirsch or Grand Marnier to taste. The biscuits in the supermarket refrigerator case that you bake yourself are quite good. So, pop them in the oven to bake while you're having dinner. Split and fill with strawberries and whipped cream.*

ONE-MINUTE SALMON

salt and pepper to taste
¾ pound salmon, sliced into thin "scallops" (see Note)
lemon wedges

Preheat oven to 550°. Lightly butter 2 heatproof dishes.

Sprinkle plates with salt and pepper. Arrange salmon in a single layer on plates and let come to room temperature. Bake for about 1½ minutes, or until fish is pale but still rose-colored at the center. Remove from oven. The heat of the plate will continue to cook the fish. Serve with lemon wedges.

NOTE: *Have your fishmonger slice the "scallops" for you. You end up with slices like smoked salmon.*

On FISH . . .

1. *Use tweezers to remove bones from fish.*
2. *Fish fillets don't need to be turned over if they are broiled.*
3. *Remove fish odors from hands by rubbing them with lemon juice.*

Cook it once—serve it twice

Go a little overboard and make twice as much as you can eat for one night's dinner. Then turn those leftovers into a completely different meal—maybe even one that is more special the second time around than the first! Whether you call them second helpings or leftovers, they are ideal for our hectic busy lifestyles.

MENU ONE	MENU TWO
GRILLED SALMON STEAK	SALMON HASH
DILLY BOILED POTATOES	SALSA
STEAMED CUCUMBERS	SLICED AVOCADO
LEMON ICE	PECAN PIE
CHARDONNAY	WHITE WINE SANGRIA SPRITZER

Fish can be wonderfully versatile for leftovers. Night one: Grill or broil 1½ to 2 pounds salmon and save half for the second night's dinner. In addition, boil 4 to 8 potatoes (depending on their size) and put half aside for the second night.

Wonderful salsas can be bought in bottles in the supermarket. They make a great accompaniment for both the Salmon Hash and the avocado.

For a sweet ending serve generous slices of store-bought pecan pie.

SALMON HASH

1½ cups cooked
    salmon, flaked
2 potatoes, boiled, cut
    into ½-inch dice
2 tablespoons minced
    bell peppers
    (assortment of red,
    green, and yellow)
¼ cup chopped onion
pinch cayenne pepper
salt and pepper to taste
1 clove garlic, crushed
2 tablespoons minced
    fresh parsley
3 tablespoons olive oil
¼ cup heavy cream

In a bowl combine salmon, potatoes, peppers, onion, cayenne, salt and pepper, garlic, and parsley.

In a heavy skillet heat olive oil. Add salmon mixture and flatten with back of spatula. When the hash begins to develop a crust on the bottom, flip over with a spatula. Add cream and turn up the heat to thicken the cream and brown the hash quickly.

Garnish with avocado and add salsa to taste.

ON LEFTOVER POSSIBILITIES...

DAY ONE	DAY TWO
Roast chicken	*Chicken potpie*
Leg of lamb	*Moussaka*
Broiled steak	*Beef tortillas*
Rice pilaf	*Fried rice*
Steamed new potatoes	*Potato salad*
Marinated tomatoes	
and mozzarella	*Pizza!*
French bread	*Bread pudding*

TONIGHT'S BARBECUE NIGHT

MENU

GINGER-LIME SWORDFISH ∨∨∨

RAW FENNEL SALAD WITH PARMESAN SHARDS ......

GRILLED PEASANT BREAD ∿∿∿

WATERMELON WEDGES ⋘⋘

BEVERAGE: DRY, MEDIUM-BODIED WHITE WINE ⋙⋙

*T*his preparation begins with assembling and marinating the swordfish. Then, move on to the fennel salad. Trim 2 fennel bulbs and slice ¼ inch thick. Toss with some lemon juice, olive oil, salt, and pepper. Using a vegetable peeler, make thin Parmesan shards from a block of Parmesan (or sprinkle with grated Parmesan). Slice ½-inch-thick pieces of peasant or French bread, brush with olive oil, and grill with the swordfish. Turn during cooking to get those great grill marks!

For dessert serve watermelon wedges with a slice of lime.

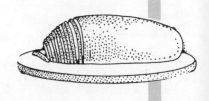

GINGER-LIME SWORDFISH

2 tablespoons peanut or
  olive oil
2 tablespoons soy sauce
2 tablespoons lime juice
2 quarter-size slices
  ginger
1 teaspoon grated lime
  zest
black pepper to taste

¾ pound swordfish
  steak, 1 inch thick

Prepare coals for grilling.

Place oil in small shallow dish. Whisk in soy sauce and lime juice. Add ginger, lime zest, and pepper to taste. Marinate swordfish in this mixture, turning occasionally, for 20 minutes.

Grill over a hot fire for 4 to 5 minutes, basting occasionally with marinade. Turn and cook for 4 to 5 minutes more, or until desired doneness. You can also cook it in the broiler 4 inches below heating element.

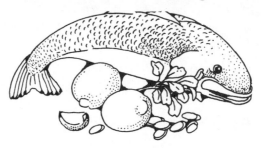

ON GRILLING FISH...

1. *Before placing fish on the grill, oil the grill first to keep the skin from sticking.*
2. *Fish can be steamed on the grill. Place fish in aluminum foil, season with butter, herbs, and white wine; seal. Place 4 to 5 inches above a medium-hot fire and cook until done.*
3. *When grilling fish, throw sprigs of fennel or thyme directly on the coals. Lightly baste the fish with a mixture of lemon juice and olive oil. The fish takes on a wonderful smoky flavor from the herbs.*

B*egin by preparing the fire (or lighting the broiler). Assemble the tuna with marinade. Slice one cucumber thinly, sprinkle lightly with salt, and let drain in a colander. Place in a serving bowl and toss with 1 tablespoon lime juice. Place the mushrooms on skewers. Shiitakes are wonderful grilled, but you can also use fresh domestic mushrooms. Brush with some olive oil and grill with the tuna.*

For dessert serve fresh pineapple sprinkled with kirsch.

LIGHT AND SPICY DINNER

MENU

TUNA STEAK WITH CORIANDER SAUCE

CUCUMBERS WITH LIME

GRILLED MUSHROOMS

FRESH PINEAPPLE WITH KIRSCH

BEVERAGE: BEER

TUNA STEAK WITH CORIANDER SAUCE

2 tablespoons minced
   green onion
2 tablespoons minced
   fresh ginger
½ cup white wine
   vinegar
2 tablespoons soy sauce
black pepper to taste
juice of 1 lime
2 tablespoons sesame
   oil
½ cup olive oil
¾ pound tuna steak
½ cup chopped
   coriander leaves
½ teaspoon black
   mustard seeds

Prepare coals for grilling.

In a shallow dish combine green onion, ginger, vinegar, soy sauce, pepper, lime, sesame and olive oils. Add tuna and marinate while assembling rest of dinner. Remove from marinade and grill over hot fire or broil until medium rare.

Heat marinade in small saucepan. Stir in coriander and mustard seeds and serve over tuna steaks.

N O T E : *Tuna is best when slightly underdone. I like to make extra of this dish because leftovers make fabulous tuna salad.*

ON MARINATING...

1. *Do not marinate fish for more than 1 hour.*
2. *To speed up marinating when short on time, place the marinade in a glass bowl. In a microwave oven heat on HIGH for 1 minute per cup of marinade to warm. Add meat, chicken, fish or vegetables to warm marinade and let stand for 30 minutes.*

MICRO MENU

MENU

RED SNAPPER WITH
BLACK BEANS AND
GINGER ~~~

CARROT AND SNOW
PEA SAUTÉ ....

CHINESE RICE ^ ^ ^ ^

MANDARIN
CHOCOLATE ICE
CREAM ......

BEVERAGE:
CHINESE BEER ◆◆◆◆◆

This snapper dish cooks in no time in the microwave so everything should be assembled and set to go before you put the snapper in the oven. It can also be prepared in a conventional oven.

Julienne the snow peas and carrots and sauté in a mixture of safflower and sesame oils. Assemble the red snapper and set aside. Then start to cook the rice and put the snapper in the oven when the rice is partially cooked. While the snapper is cooking set the table.

For dessert serve chocolate ice cream garnished with drained mandarin oranges.

RED SNAPPER WITH BLACK BEANS AND GINGER

2 pound whole red snapper, cleaned but leave on head and tail
2 cloves garlic, minced
3 quarter-size pieces ginger, julienned
2 tablespoons Chinese fermented black beans (see Note)
2 tablespoons minced fresh coriander
2 green onions, sliced
3 tablespoons soy sauce
1 tablespoon sesame oil
1 tablespoon rice wine vinegar

Slash fish on the diagonal in 2 places on each side. Put on a large platter or oval gratin dish. Sprinkle garlic, ginger, black beans, coriander, and green onions on top. In small bowl combine soy sauce, sesame oil, and rice wine vinegar. Pour over fish and cover with plastic wrap. Cook on HIGH for 11 minutes. Remove head and tail and serve.

To cook snapper in a conventional oven, arrange as directed above in an ovenproof oval gratin dish. Pour a mixture of ½ cup white wine and ½ cup water around fish in dish. Bring almost to the simmer on top of stove, lay a piece of buttered wax paper on top of fish, and put in a preheated 350° oven to cook for 10 minutes per inch of thickness of fish, measured at its thickest point.

N O T E : *The fermented black beans are available in oriental groceries or some supermarkets.*

PERFECT FISH IN THE MICROWAVE...

1. *Arrange the fish fillets in a baking dish with the thickest parts pointing outward; microwave on HIGH for 3 minutes per pound of boneless fish.*
2. *Cover the dish with wax paper.*
3. *When poaching or steaming fish, seal with plastic wrap.*
4. *When microwaving a whole fish, shield the head and tail with aluminum foil to prevent overcooking.*
5. *For sauce-based recipes, microwave the sauce first, then add the fish.*

SAUTÉED AND SIMPLE

MENU

FILLET OF SOLE WITH
PECAN CRUST

SPINACH SALAD

BOWL OF CHERRIES

BUTTER COOKIES

BEVERAGE:
ICED TEA

For this menu prepare sole up to the point of actually cooking it and set aside while you assemble the spinach salad. Wash 2 handfuls of spinach and dry. Combine in a bowl with julienned Swiss cheese and sliced fresh mushrooms. Toss with 4 tablespoons olive oil, 2 tablespoons red wine vinegar, salt and pepper to taste, and ½ teaspoon mustard. For dessert serve an icy bowl of cherries accompanied by butter cookies.

FILLET OF SOLE WITH PECAN CRUST

½ cup pecans
¾ pound fillet of sole
1 egg white, beaten
    until frothy
2 tablespoons vegetable
    oil
3 tablespoons butter
2 teaspoons lemon juice
1 tablespoon minced
    fresh parsley

In a food processor chop pecans finely, being careful not to puree. Brush fish with some of egg white and coat with pecans, pressing into fish with fingertips.

In a skillet (preferably nonstick) heat oil and 1 tablespoon butter. Add fish and cook until golden brown, about 3 minutes. Turn and cook for another 2 minutes. Remove to a platter and discard any fat remaining in pan.

Heat remaining 2 tablespoons butter in skillet, add lemon juice and parsley. Serve over fish.

NUTTY FACTS...

DID YOU KNOW . . .

10-ounce bag = 2½ cups

1 pound bag in the shell = 2 cups shelled

4 ounce can = 1 cup

1 pound bag = 4 cups

ON SPINACH...

1. *Fresh spinach is quite perishable. Store it in a sealed plastic bag in the vegetable crisper and use it within a day or two.*
2. *Frozen spinach can easily be substituted for fresh in most recipes, excluding, of course, things like spinach salad.*

SEAFARING DINNER

MENU

MARINER MUSSELS

SOURDOUGH
BAGUETTES

STRAWBERRY ICE
CREAM

BEVERAGE:
SPICY TOMATO JUICE
COCKTAIL

These mussels produce their own "soup." If you add baguettes for sopping up the soup, you have a filling enough meal for even the biggest appetite.
Serve strawberry ice cream for dessert.

Mariner Mussels

2½ pounds mussels
¼ cup cornmeal
1 tablespoon olive oil
¼ cup minced onions
2 cloves garlic, minced
½ bay leaf
1 teaspoon dried thyme
4 sprigs parsley
⅔ cup dry white wine

Scrub mussels clean with a brush, and pull off beards. To further clean mussels, put them in a bowl and add cornmeal. Fill bowl with water and let sit for at least 15 minutes. Mussels will feed on cornmeal and disgorge any sand. Rinse and drain.

Heat olive oil in a large skillet with high sides and a tight-fitting lid. Add onions, garlic, bay leaf, and thyme, and sauté for 5 minutes. Add parsley, white wine, and bring to the boil. Boil for 2 minutes. Add mussels, cover tightly, and cook over medium-high heat for 5 minutes, or until shells have opened.

Serve mussels and cooking liquid in soup bowls.

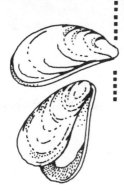

On Quick Desserts...

1. *In a bowl combine blueberries and strawberries with a little Galliano liqueur. Serve over vanilla ice cream.*
2. *Combine plain yogurt with honey or brown sugar to taste and serve as a topping for grapes, sliced peaches, or nectarines.*
3. *Keep fan-shaped wafers on hand to dress up a goblet of ice cream or sorbet.*
4. *Combine vanilla yogurt and fresh blackberries for a refreshing dessert.*

SOMETHING OUT OF NOTHING

MENU

MARINATED
ROASTED PEPPERS

SHRIMP CREOLE

RICE

DRIED FRUIT
COMPOTE

BEVERAGE:
BEER

This menu takes full advantage of the short order cook's pantry of staples. You should be able to complete this dinner without a trip to the supermarket. What a treat! Both the peppers and fruit in this menu can be made ahead of time and kept in the refrigerator.

To save time . . .

Buy bottled roasted peppers and arrange them in a serving dish. Top with anchovies, salt and pepper to taste, and oregano. Add vinegar and enough olive oil to cover. Marinate in refrigerator.

FRUIT COMPOTE: vvvvvvvvvvvvvvvvvvv vvvvvvvvvvvvvvvvvv

Bring to a boil ¼ cup sugar, ½ cup dark rum, 1 cup water, and 1 vanilla bean. Simmer uncovered for 5 minutes, add 4 ounces dried fruit, and cook for 20 minutes. Chill until ready to serve. If desired, top with whipped cream or ice cream.

Shrimp Creole

In skillet melt butter and sauté mushrooms until softened; remove to a side dish. Add flour to pan, stir to combine with remaining butter and cook for 3 minutes. Add barbecue sauce, tomatoes, onion, salt, and thyme. Bring to the boil. Lower heat, cover, and simmer for 15 minutes. Add shrimp and mushrooms. Cook for 10 minutes more.

Serve over rice.

2 tablespoons butter
½ cup button
    mushrooms
2 tablespoons flour
¼ cup barbecue sauce
1 cup canned plum
    tomatoes
¼ cup thinly sliced
    onion
½ teaspoon salt
pinch thyme
¾ pound cooked baby
    shrimp

On Roasted Peppers...

If you can't find bottled roasted peppers, here's how to roast peppers yourself:

Use metal tongs to hold a whole red pepper over the gas flame, turning frequently. Cook the pepper until charred and blackened all over. Put in a tightly closed brown paper bag to steam for 5 minutes. Scrape the skin off the pepper with the blunt edge of a knife.

If doing a number of peppers, it is easier to place them on a foil-lined baking sheet and broil, turning, until done.

STATE o' MAINE DINNER

MENU

▼▼▼▼ CRAB CAKES WITH
      TARTAR SAUCE

〜〜 COLE SLAW

○ ○ ○ CORN-ON-THE-COB

﹀﹀﹀﹀ PEACH ICE CREAM

ᵹ ᵹ ᵹ ᵹ BEVERAGE:
         FROSTY MUG OF
         BEER

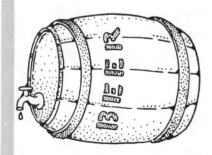

This menu makes me think of summertime and fresh breezes. Assemble the crab cakes first and put them in the refrigerator. Bring water to the boil for corn and then fry the crab cakes and cook the corn. Serve scoops of peach ice cream for dessert.

CRAB CAKES WITH TARTAR SAUCE

Place crabmeat in mixing bowl. Cover with bread crumbs and pour milk over all. In a small bowl combine ½ egg, mayonnaise, Worcestershire sauce, dry mustard, baking powder, parsley, salt, and pepper. Add to crab mixture and stir to combine. Form into 4 to 6 crab cakes and place on a plate in refrigerator for 20 minutes.

In a heavy skillet heat butter and vegetable oil. Dredge crab cakes lightly in flour, shaking off excess, and sauté until golden, turning once.

½ pound crabmeat
½ cup bread crumbs
2½ tablespoons milk
1 egg, lightly beaten (only use half)
2 tablespoons mayonnaise
¼ teaspoon Worcestershire sauce
¼ teaspoon dry mustard
¼ teaspoon baking powder
1 tablespoon minced fresh parsley
¼ teaspoon salt
white pepper to taste
2 tablespoons butter
1 tablespoon vegetable oil
flour

BEST HOMEMADE TARTAR SAUCE ▼▼▼▼▼▼▼▼▼▼▼▼▼▼▼▼▼

½ cup mayonnaise
¼ cup sour cream
¼ teaspoon Dijon mustard
1½ teaspoons minced gherkin
½ teaspoon minced fresh parsley
2 teaspoons minced fresh dill
pinch dried tarragon
dash Tabasco sauce
salt and pepper to taste

Whisk together all ingredients in a bowl. *Makes ¾ cup.*

ON CORN...

1. *After corn is shucked, remove any excess silk clinging to the kernels by rubbing with a moistened paper towel.*
2. *Corn kernels toughen if you add salt to the boiling water at the beginning of the cooking.*
3. *Cover the cooking pot. This traps steam, which will cook any corn not submerged in water.*
4. *Small amounts of leftover corn may be added to pancake or muffin batter for variety.*

IT'S A BREEZE DINNER FOR TWO

MENU

SOUTH BREEZE SCALLOPS

STEAMED GREEN BEANS

PARSLIED PILAF

VANILLA ICE CREAM WITH OREO COOKIES

BEVERAGE: DRY, MEDIUM-BODIED WHITE WINE

Mallory Finger's scallop dish is a "breeze" to make! Prepare the scallops up to the point where they are arranged in a dish with butter drizzled on top. Set aside. Next, prepare your own favorite rice pilaf recipe using ½ cup rice and 1 cup liquid. Add 2 tablespoons chopped parsley when it's finished cooking. Begin to broil the scallops while the rice is cooking; steam the green beans for 8 minutes, or until desired tenderness; and open the wine. After dinner, scoop out the vanilla ice cream and open the box of Oreos.

SOUTH BREEZE SCALLOPS

Preheat broiler.

Wash scallops and dry well. In a small saucepan melt butter, add garlic, and cook on low heat for 5 minutes. Add parsley, Marsala or sherry, lemon juice, salt and pepper. Heat for a few minutes. In a bowl combine bread crumbs and Parmesan, and set aside.

Place scallops in an ovenproof shallow dish and pour butter mixture over scallops. Broil, uncovered, for 4 minutes. Stir scallops, turn them over, and broil for 4 minutes more. Sprinkle bread-crumb mixture on top of scallops. Broil for 3 minutes, or until topping is lightly browned.

¾ pound bay scallops
   (or sea scallops cut
   in half)
2 tablespoons butter
2 cloves garlic, crushed
1 tablespoon minced
   fresh parsley
3 tablespoons dry
   Marsala or dry
   sherry
2 tablespoons lemon
   juice
salt and pepper to taste
½ cup bread crumbs
¼ cup grated Parmesan
   cheese

ON OTHER QUICK DESSERTS...

1. *Try warm maple syrup with walnut halves. Pour over some vanilla ice cream and serve with chocolate-covered biscuit fingers.*
2. *Have a slice of store-bought pound cake garnished with fresh raspberries.*
3. *Lightly moisten the underside of ladyfingers with dark rum or brandy. Sandwich 2 ladyfingers with good-quality chocolate pudding or store-bought chocolate mousse. You can also moisten them with kirsch or framboise and sandwich with bottled lemon curd. Sieve powdered sugar on top.*

POULTRY

SIZZLING SOUTHWEST DINNER

MENU

GUACAMOLE WITH
TACO CHIPS

CORNISH HENS WITH
CHILI BUTTER

VEGETABLE MEDLEY

BLUEBERRY-FILLED
PAPAYA HALVES

BEVERAGE:
THE PERFECT
MARGARITA

This spicy-hot Southwest menu will actually help cool you off, especially when served with icy Margaritas to fan the flames! You can buy guacamole and taco chips at the supermarket (guacamole is usually in the freezer case). If you like, the hens can be assembled the night before and left in the refrigerator (bring to room temperature before cooking). Put them under the broiler just before dinner is to be served.

The vegetable medley is an assortment of fresh or frozen veggies made up of cooked zucchini and corn kernels tossed with chopped tomatoes, butter, salt, and pepper. For dessert peel a papaya, slice it in half lengthwise, and fill the halves with blueberries. Garnish with sprigs of mint.

CORNISH HENS WITH CHILI BUTTER

Preheat broiler.

In a small bowl use a fork to mash together butter, chili powder, salt, and garlic until smooth. Set aside.

Place hens breast side up in a shallow roasting pan and, using your fingers, carefully lift breast skin away from the flesh. With a spoon spread some chili butter under the skin on both sides of the breastbone. Also rub chili butter on top of the skin. Repeat with remaining hen.

Broil 5 inches from heat, skin side down, for 10 minutes. Turn hens and, basting occasionally, continue broiling for about 10 minutes more, or until juices run clear when hen is pricked with a fork.

5 tablespoons butter
1½ teaspoons hot chili powder
½ teaspoon salt
1 clove garlic, minced
2 Cornish hens, split down the back and flattened

THE PERFECT MARGARITA

lime peel

coarse salt

1½ ounces tequila

1½ ounces Cointreau

1½ ounces lime juice

Rub rim of 8-ounce glass with lime peel. Put coarse salt on flat dish. Turn glass upside down and press rim into salt. Fill with ice. Add tequila, Cointreau, and lime juice and stir to combine. *Serves 1.*

ON BROILING...

1. *In order for meat to sear properly, bring to room temperature before cooking and preheat the broiler and broiling pan.*
2. *Make sure the meat is dry before broiling.*
3. *Brush vegetable oil on the broiler pan before using.*
4. *Broiling gives you the same crisp skin as oven roasting but in less time.*

ELEGANT BARBECUE FOR TWO

MENU

GRILLED CORNISH GAME HENS ~~~

GRILLED VEGETABLES ▮▮▮▮▮

SHORTBREAD AND JAM SANDWICH ○ ○ ○

BEVERAGE: LEMONADE ℓℓℓℓℓ

*T*he hens should be marinated overnight if you have the time. Prepare the evening before. Grilled vegetables should be an assortment, choosing from tomato, onion, squash, zucchini, eggplant, mushrooms, or whatever you like. Cut them into ½-inch slices and thread on skewers. Season with salt and pepper. Grill over a fire, basting with olive oil and turning until softened and browned. Splash *with a little red wine vinegar before serving. For dessert spread the top of 2 shortbread cookies with strawberry jam. Lay 2 more cookies on top, forming "sandwiches."*

GRILLED CORNISH GAME HENS

¾ cup plain yogurt
1½ tablespoons honey
1 tablespoon ground
    cumin
2 teaspoons dry mustard
2 1-pound Cornish hens

In a shallow dish mix together yogurt, honey, cumin, and mustard.

Split hens by cutting down backbone and flattening breastbone with the palm of your hand. Place in a dish with yogurt mixture. Turn to coat hens. Refrigerate overnight. Remove from marinade and grill over a hot fire for 30 to 35 minutes, turning once, or until juices run clear when pricked with a fork. These can also be done in the broiler.

NOTE : *These hens can be broiled 5 minutes on each side and then baked at 450° for 30 minutes.*

ON CORNISH HENS...

1. *Cornish hens are a good choice because they take less time to cook than a whole chicken.*

2. *Cut down backbone and flatten the breastbone with the palm of your hand so it will lie flat and cook evenly.*

CELEBRATE SPRING!

MENU

CHICKEN BREASTS
WITH TWO
MUSTARDS

STEAMED NEW
POTATOES

ASPARAGUS WITH
LEMON VINAIGRETTE

RHUBARB PIE

BEVERAGE:
CHILLED DRY ROSÉ

Spring often makes me think about asparagus and rhubarb —just to name a few foods of the season. Bring 2 pots of water to the boil for potatoes and asparagus while you start to prepare the chicken. Steam new potatoes and toss with a little butter and fresh herbs. Blanch asparagus and serve warm with a lemon vinaigrette dressing. For dessert stop at the bakery for a fresh rhubarb pie.

CHICKEN BREASTS WITH TWO MUSTARDS

2 whole chicken
    breasts, boned but
    with skin left on
salt and pepper to taste
2 tablespoons butter,
    melted
2 tablespoons Dijon
    mustard
2 tablespoons coarse-
    grained French
    mustard
¼ teaspoon dried
    tarragon
1 tablespoon bread
    crumbs combined
    with 1 tablespoon
    chopped walnuts or
    pecans

Preheat broiler. Line broiler pan with foil for easier cleanup. Place breasts on foil, skin side up. Season with salt and pepper. Drizzle with half of melted butter. Broil until skin starts to brown, about 5 minutes.

In a small bowl combine mustards and tarragon. Brush over skin sides of breasts. Drizzle with remaining butter. Sprinkle with bread-crumb mixture. Continue broiling until lightly browned, 2 to 3 minutes. Reduce oven temperature to 400°. Bake until cooked through (chicken should be slightly springy to the touch), 5 to 12 minutes (depending on size of breasts).

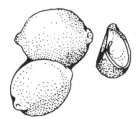

ON LEMONS...

1. *Don't slice into a lemon when you need only a few drops. Instead, puncture it with a toothpick, squeeze out what you need and store in refrigerator with a toothpick.*
2. *For highest juice yield, have lemons at room temperature before squeezing, or microwave on HIGH for 30 seconds.*

ON RHUBARB...

Buy when in season, trim off leafy tops (they are poisonous), and cut in cubes. Store in an airtight container in the freezer. This way you can enjoy rhubarb out of season.

Easy Chicken Dinner

MENU

SHERRY-MUSHROOM CHICKEN ^ ^ ^

ARTICHOKE HEARTS ●‖●‖●

BUTTERED NOODLES ▪ ▪ ▪

AMARETTI CRUMBLE ○ ○ ○

BEVERAGE:
DRY MEDIUM-BODIED
WHITE WINE

Assemble the chicken and put in the oven first. Bring 2 pots of water to the boil for the noodles and frozen artichoke hearts.
For dessert crumble amaretti cookies and moisten with dark rum. Serve as a topping for coffee ice cream.

SHERRY-MUSHROOM CHICKEN

1 10¾-oz. can cream of
    mushroom soup
1 cup sour cream
2 tablespoons flour
½ cup dry sherry
2 teaspoons dried
    oregano
2 teaspoons dried
    tarragon
1 clove garlic, minced
black pepper to taste
2 whole boneless,
    skinless chicken
    breasts, halved

Preheat oven to 350°. Grease shallow baking pan.

In a bowl combine all ingredients, except chicken. Place chicken in baking dish, in single layer. Pour soup mixture over top. Bake for 30 minutes.

ON CHICKEN...

1. *Make sure to wash the cutting surface, utensils, and your hands well after working with chicken.*
2. *Tie together several sprigs of fresh rosemary or thyme to use as a basting brush for roasted or grilled chicken.*
3. *When breading chicken (or anything else), keep one hand dry just in case the phone rings!*

STEAM HEAT SSSS!

MENU

CHICKEN AND SCALLION MEDALLIONS ON A BED OF SPROUTS

SAUTÉED BABY SPINACH

ASSORTED JAPANESE PICKLES

RASPBERRY SORBET WITH CHOCOLATE SHAVINGS

BEVERAGE: JAPANESE BEER

The medallions in this menu make a fabulous main course salad and can be served warm or at room temperature. They are also wonderfully versatile and can even be served as hors d'oeuvres! Sauté fresh spinach in a covered skillet with some olive oil and crushed garlic until wilted. Japanese pickles can be found in gourmet stores and even some supermarkets. For dessert serve raspberry sorbet topped with chocolate shavings.

CHICKEN AND SCALLION MEDALLIONS ON A BED OF SPROUTS

2 whole skinless,
    boneless chicken
    breasts, halved
salt and pepper to taste
4–8 scallions, white part
    only
½ cup soy sauce
4 tablespoons white
    wine vinegar
3 cups bean sprouts

Between 2 sheets of wax paper flatten chicken breasts using a mallet or the back of a frying pan to ⅛ inch thick.

Lay each breast, skin side down, on work surface and sprinkle with salt and pepper. Arrange scallions lengthwise along side of each breast (you may need to use 2 scallions, end to end). Tightly roll up chicken, jelly-roll fashion, tucking in ends. Tie chicken in 2 places with kitchen string to hold closed.

In bowl combine soy sauce and vinegar. Add chicken and turn to coat with marinade. Set aside for 15 minutes (longer if time permits).

In a skillet or steamer bring ½ inch of water to the boil. Place a wire rack in skillet, clearing the water, and place chicken rolls on the rack. Cover and steam for 15 minutes, turning once. While steaming, bring marinade to boil in saucepan and simmer for 2 minutes.

When rolls are cooked, remove string and slice at an angle into ½-inch pieces. Arrange on a bed of bean sprouts and pour warm marinade over.

ON STEAMING...

1. *Steaming is one of the most nutritious methods of cooking and, as an added bonus, it seals in flavor, color, and texture.*
2. *Steaming can be done with an improvised rack, as described in the Chicken and Scallion Medallions recipe, with a metal vegetable steaming basket, or in a bamboo steamer.*

THANKSGIVING THE SECOND TIME AROUND

MENU

TURKEY CROUSTADES

STEAMED GREEN BEANS

CRANBERRY SAUCE

BROILED GRAPEFRUIT

BEVERAGE: DRY, LIGHT-BODIED WHITE WINE

This main course will give new life to your turkey leftovers. Put the croustades in to bake while preparing the turkey filling. For dessert prepare and serve pink grapefruit halves, topped with a sprinkling of brown sugar, and browned briefly under the broiler.

TURKEY CROUSTADES

1 loaf unsliced white
bread
3 tablespoons butter,
plus 2 tablespoons
melted
¼ pound mushrooms,
sliced
½ cup thinly sliced
onion
3 tablespoons flour
1½ cups chicken stock
1½ teaspoons dried
tarragon
salt and pepper to taste
2 tablespoons heavy
cream or milk
2 tablespoons minced
fresh parsley
1½ cups cubed cooked
turkey
2 carrots, peeled, thinly
sliced

Preheat oven to 375°.

Cut two 1½-inch-thick slices from bread and remove crusts. Use remaining loaf for sandwiches. With a small sharp knife, hollow out each slice of bread halfway down, leaving sides ¼ inch thick to make a shell. Brush all over with the 2 tablespoons melted butter. Bake on a cookie sheet for 10 to 15 minutes, or until golden.

In a saucepan melt the 3 tablespoons butter. Add mushrooms and onion. Sauté for 5 minutes. Add flour. Cook, while stirring, for 1 minute. Slowly whisk in chicken stock. Bring to the boil to thicken, then reduce heat to simmering. Add tarragon, salt and pepper, and cream or milk. Simmer for 5 minutes. Add parsley, turkey, and carrots and simmer for 5 minutes more. Spoon filling into baked croustades.

ON LEFTOVER STUFFING...

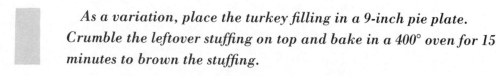

As a variation, place the turkey filling in a 9-inch pie plate. Crumble the leftover stuffing on top and bake in a 400° oven for 15 minutes to brown the stuffing.

MEAT

GREEN AS A FIELD VEAL CHOPS

*P*repare 2 artichokes for the microwave by trimming and wrapping individually in plastic wrap. Set aside. Next, make the arugula stuffing and put the artichokes in the microwave during the last 15 minutes of cooking the veal. Cook on HIGH for 5 to 9 minutes, depending on size of artichokes, and let stand for 5 minutes. Unwrap and serve with butter and salt. If you don't have a microwave, use frozen artichoke hearts cooked according to the package directions.

For dessert serve almond cookies with café filtre.

MENU

VEAL CHOPS WITH ARUGULA STUFFING

BUTTERED ARTICHOKES

ALMOND COOKIES

CAFÉ FILTRE

BEVERAGE: RICH, FULL-BODIED RED WINE

VEAL CHOPS WITH ARUGULA STUFFING

3 tablespoons butter
3 tablespoons minced
    shallots
1 bunch arugula (2
    cups), chopped
1 ounce goat cheese,
    crumbled
1 ounce cream cheese,
    cubed
salt and pepper to taste
¼ teaspoon dried thyme
2 rib veal chops, about 1
    inch thick
1 tablespoon vegetable
    oil
flour

In a skillet melt 1 tablespoon butter. Add shallots and sauté for 3 minutes, until softened. Add arugula and sauté for 2 minutes, until wilted. Remove to a mixing bowl. Add goat cheese, cream cheese, salt and pepper, and thyme. Stir and mash to combine. Set aside to cool slightly.

Cut a 2-inch pocket horizontally in each veal chop. Fill each with arugula stuffing and press pocket together to enclose filling.

In a skillet melt remaining 2 tablespoons butter with vegetable oil. Dredge chops in flour, shaking off excess. Add chops to skillet and brown for 5 minutes on each side. Lower heat and cook for 15 minutes, covered, turning once, until cooked through.

ON ADVANCE PREPARATION...

The more you do in advance, the better. You just have to plan ahead. For example, I have one friend who does her cooking at 6:00 A.M. because she's an early riser and her family isn't up and about yet. Cooking can be quite therapeutic if you're not rushed, so find your best time.

Some things to do ahead:

1. *Peel the potatoes and soak in water.*
2. *Trim and blanch the vegetables.*
3. *Wash the salad greens.*
4. *Start marinating.*
5. *Prepare the piecrust.*
6. *Set the table.*
7. *Grate the cheese.*

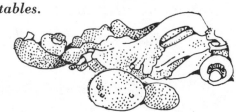

TOAST THE GOOD OLD DAYS

MENU

JANE'S VEAL SCALLOPINI WITH WHITE WINE AND MUSHROOMS

BUTTERED ZUCCHINI SHAVINGS

STEAMED BABY NEW POTATOES

CHOCOLATE CAKE

BEVERAGE: DRY, LIGHT-BODIED WHITE WINE

This veal recipe is on a recipe card of mine quite spattered from use over the years. It comes from Jane Mitchell, my college roommate, and was one of the first dishes I learned how to cook. Even though veal scallopini is an expensive cut, you only need ½ pound for 2 people, which makes it more affordable.

First, bring a pot of water to the boil for the potatoes and begin steaming the potatoes while you start cooking the veal. Done at the last moment, the zucchini shavings are a quick stir-fry of grated zucchini in butter with salt, pepper, and oregano. For dessert serve chocolate cake from the bakery. My friend Jane and I used to sit on the floor in the dormitory hallway and eat Sarah Lee Chocolate Cake right from the box. We've both come a long way since then!

JANE'S VEAL SCALLOPINI WITH WHITE WINE AND MUSHROOMS

4 tablespoons butter
1 tablespoon vegetable oil
½ pound thin veal scallopini
flour
salt and pepper to taste
¼ pound mushrooms, thinly sliced
6 tablespoons chicken stock
½ cup dry white wine
juice of 1 lemon

Put 2 tablespoons butter and 1 tablespoon vegetable oil in a large skillet and heat over high heat. Dredge the veal in flour, shaking off excess, and put in skillet in a single layer. Brown quickly for 1 to 2 minutes on each side. Transfer veal to a platter and season with salt and pepper. Pour fat out of skillet. Melt remaining 2 tablespoons butter in skillet and sauté mushrooms on moderate heat for 4 minutes. Add stock, white wine, lemon juice, and salt and pepper. Turn heat to high, bring liquid to the boil, and scrape up any browned bits clinging to bottom of pan. Reduce heat to simmer and return veal to pan. Cover and simmer for 1 minute. Serve immediately.

ON POTATOES...

1. *When boiling potatoes for salad or to serve hot and buttered, add a chicken bouillon cube to the cooking water for extra flavor.*
2. *A few teaspoons of instant mashed potatoes added to overly salted gravy draws out excess salt.*

VEAL SCALLOPS WITH A SPECIAL TOUCH

*B*egin by stuffing the eggplant: Use 2 baby Italian eggplants. Slice in half lengthwise. With a knife, score diamonds into the cut sides. In a small bowl mix together some chopped parsley, garlic, salt and pepper, and enough olive oil to moisten. Poke into the incisions, drizzle with olive oil, and bake in 375° oven for 20 minutes.

While the eggplant is baking, prepare the veal chops. Serve sliced fresh plums for dessert, sprinkled with cinnamon and sugar.

MENU

SUNNY VEAL SCALLOPS

STUFFED EGGPLANT

CINNAMON-SUGAR PLUMS

BEVERAGE: RICH, FULL-BODIED RED WINE

Sunny Veal Scallops

¾ cup bread crumbs
½ cup grated Parmesan
   cheese
zest of 1 lemon
½ teaspoon salt
pinch black pepper
1 egg
½ pound veal scallopini
¼ cup flour
3 tablespoons olive oil

In a bowl combine bread crumbs, Parmesan, lemon zest, salt, and pepper. In another bowl beat egg.

Dredge veal in flour, shaking off excess. Dip veal in egg and then in bread-crumb mixture.

In a large skillet heat olive oil. Add veal and sauté for 2 to 3 minutes on each side, until browned.

On Grocery Shopping...

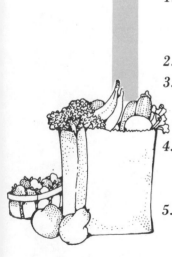

1. *Keep a piece of paper near the refrigerator and have a grocery list in the works at all times. Just continue adding to the list when you run out of items.*
2. *Once a month do a big grocery shop for staple items.*
3. *Plan menus for the week on Tuesday. That way you can shop on Wednesday, the day when markets seem to be well stocked and you can shop for your week's menu in just one trip.*
4. *Take advantage of the ready-prepared foods in the market. It could be fresh-squeezed orange juice, cut-up salad ingredients, or even a full main course.*
5. *In New York (and I'm sure in other big cities) you can even call in your grocery list to the supermarket and have everything delivered without even venturing to the market.*

MENU

VEAL SCALLOPINI
WITH MARSALA
WINE SAUCE ••••

ORZO WITH PEAS
AND ONIONS ooo

GRAHAM CRACKERS
SUPREME ⟨⟨⟨⟨

BEVERAGE:
RICH, FULL-BODIED
RED WINE ▲▲▲▲

*P*repare orzo according to the package directions. Also prepare frozen peas and onions, and drain. Stir the two together. While they are cooking, prepare the veal. For dessert arrange graham crackers on a baking sheet. Top each with 1 tablespoon chocolate chips. Bake in a 350° oven for 3 to 5 minutes, or until the chips are soft. Use a knife to spread the chocolate evenly on each cracker. Top with some chopped walnuts and set aside to cool briefly.
Serve this meal in the library or den, for a change, instead of in the kitchen or dining room.

VEAL SCALLOPINI WITH MARSALA WINE SAUCE

1 egg beaten with 1
    tablespoon water
⅓ cup bread crumbs
⅓ cup grated Parmesan
    cheese
½ pound veal scallopini
¼ cup flour
4 tablespoons butter
1 tablespoon vegetable
    oil
1 tablespoon minced
    fresh parsley
2 tablespoons lemon
    juice
⅓ cup Marsala

Place egg mixture in a bowl. In another bowl combine bread crumbs and cheese. Dust veal with flour, shaking off excess. Dip veal in egg and roll in crumb mixture. Place on wax paper and refrigerate for 10 minutes.

In a skillet melt 2 tablespoons butter with oil. Add veal and sauté for 3 to 5 minutes, turning once, or until veal is springy. Remove to a warm platter. In same skillet melt remaining 2 tablespoons butter. Add parsley, lemon juice, and Marsala. Bring to the boil, scraping up browned particles in pan. Return veal to pan to warm with sauce.

Variation: This same preparation can also be done with flattened boneless, skinless chicken breasts.

ON KITCHEN TIMING...

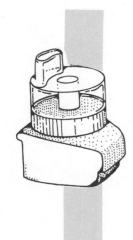

1. *Start by cooking whatever will take the longest first.*
2. *Begin preheating the oven when you walk into the kitchen.*
3. *Start with hot tap water when you need a pot of boiling water and keep the cover on to trap the steam.*
4. *If you have the room, try to keep your timesaving appliances (i.e., food processor) on the countertop. You can get at them faster and will want to use them more often.*
5. *Think about when to use a pressure cooker to save time.*
6. *Prepare your own bottled salad dressing and store in an airtight jar in the refrigerator.*
7. *Take advantage of foul-weather days to prepare ahead and stock the freezer.*

LAMB CHOP DINNER

MENU

SAUTÉED LAMB CHOPS

MUSHROOM PILAF

BABY CARROTS WITH DILL

VANILLA ICE CREAM WITH GINGERSNAPS

BEVERAGE: MARTINIS

Begin by starting the rice pilaf and add sautéed mushrooms to it when finished cooking. Cook the carrots in a pot of boiling water. Drain and toss with a pat of butter, a few snippets of dill, salt, and pepper. While both are cooking, prepare the chops.

For dessert serve vanilla ice cream with your favorite gingersnaps.

Sautéed Lamb Chops

6 single-rib lamb chops
2 tablespoons olive oil
2 cloves garlic, peeled
salt and pepper to taste
2 teaspoons dried thyme
⅓ cup dry white wine

Flatten chops to ½ inch thick. In a large skillet heat olive oil and garlic on medium heat. When garlic turns a pale golden, discard it. Raise heat to high and add chops in a single layer. Brown for 2 minutes on the first side, turn, and brown for 1 minute more. Remove lamb chops to a platter and season with salt and pepper. Add thyme and wine to pan. Reduce to 3 tablespoons, scraping up browned bits in bottom of pan. Return chops to pan and turn over in skillet to coat with juices.

On Meat...

1. *When flouring meat before sautéing, put flour (or bread crumbs) on a paper towel to throw away afterward instead of on a plate that will need to be washed.*
2. *Partially freeze meats for easier slicing.*
3. *Dehydrated onion soup is a good flavor enhancer for meat stews.*

JULY 4TH BARBECUE CELEBRATION FOR TWO

MENU

STUFFED BURGERS
ON GARLIC BUNS

POTATO SALAD

BREAD AND BUTTER
PICKLES

WATERMELON

BEVERAGE:
BLOODY MARYS

*E*ven those people who try not to eat too much red meat (myself included) find that at least once during the summer they start dreaming about a juicy grilled hamburger. If you don't have time to wait for the grill to get hot, you can broil or pan-fry the burgers. If you want to grill and you have a gas barbecue, you are ahead of the game in the "time" department.
This technique of "stuffing" hamburgers with American

cheese was taught to me by a friend years ago. I have updated it with cheddar, but you could also use blue cheese or goat cheese. The potato salad and bread and butter pickles are store-bought, so start sipping the Bloody Marys and relax while the grill heats up!

For dessert serve juicy watermelon slices.

STUFFED BURGERS ON GARLIC BUNS

In a bowl mash together butter, garlic, and hot sauce. Spread on hamburger buns and set aside.

Shape beef into patties. Make a pocket or depression in center of each patty, fill with a chunk of cheese and re-form into patty, hiding cheese in the middle.

Broil, pan-fry, or grill burgers for 5 minutes on each side for rare, or to desired doneness. Grill buns, or toast in oven, while cooking burgers. Top with your choice of garnishes.

2 tablespoons butter
¼ teaspoon crushed
   garlic
dash of hot sauce
   (optional)
2 hamburger buns
¾ pound ground lean
   beef
2 ounces cheddar
   cheese, cut in 2
   chunks
Garnish:
lettuce
sliced tomato
sliced onion
barbecue sauce

A SIMPLE POTATO SALAD

As soon as potatoes are cool enough to handle, slice ¼ inch thick. Place potatoes and green onions in a mixing bowl.

In a screw-top jar combine vinegar, oil, salt, pepper, parsley, tarragon, and capers. Shake to combine and pour enough dressing on potatoes to moisten. Toss gently to combine.

NOTE : *This recipe can easily be made in larger quantities for larger groups.*

4 new potatoes, cooked
   and unpeeled
1 green onion, minced

DRESSING:

2 tablespoons red wine
   vinegar
¼ cup olive oil
salt and pepper, to taste
2 teaspoons minced
   fresh parsley
2 teaspoons minced,
   tarragon, or 1
   teaspoon dried
   tarragon
1 tablespoon chopped
   capers (optional)

SKILLET COOKING

MENU

SKILLET MEAT LOAF
WITH TOMATO
SAUCE

STEAMED BUTTERED
NEW POTATOES

ORANGE SECTIONS
WITH GRAND
MARNIER SPLASH

BEVERAGE:
RICH FULL-BODIED
RED WINE

This recipe from my favorite recipe developer, Janice Burne, for skillet meat loaf, cooks with its own sauce and uses the leanest beef for those of you who are health- and weight-conscious. It's perfect served with new potatoes, which can be steamed in 15 minutes and tossed with a pat of butter while the meat loaf is cooking. The red wine you drink can also be used in the tomato sauce.
For dessert peel and section 2 oranges and top with a splash of Grand Marnier.

Skillet Meat Loaf with Tomato Sauce

In a mixing bowl combine egg, Parmesan, bread crumbs, milk, garlic, onion, 2 tablespoons parsley, 1½ teaspoons basil, oregano, salt and pepper. Add ground beef and mix.

Heat vegetable oil in a large skillet. Make a large ball with ground-meat mixture and place in hot oil. Flatten meat out with the back of a spoon and brown for 5 minutes. Spoon out excess fat. Carefully turn meat over. Pour crushed tomatoes, red wine, 2 teaspoons basil, and remaining 1 tablespoon parsley over meat. Cover, lower heat, and simmer for 20 minutes. Cut into wedges and serve.

N O T E : *Leftovers are wonderful cold the next day in a sandwich.*

1 egg
3 tablespoons grated Parmesan cheese
3 tablespoons bread crumbs
¼ cup milk
1 clove garlic, minced
1 small onion, chopped
3 tablespoons minced fresh parsley
3½ teaspoons dried basil
½ teaspoon dried oregano
salt and pepper to taste
1 pound extra-lean ground beef
1 tablespoon vegetable oil
1 1-pound can crushed tomatoes
¼ cup red wine

On Oranges...

1. *Place oranges in boiling water for 5 minutes before peeling in order to make it easier to remove the white membrane.*
2. *Select oranges that are heavy for their size. They will be juicier.*
3. *Squeeze oranges at room temperature for maximum yield.*

Eat It, It's Good for You

MENU

MOM'S CALF'S LIVER AND ONIONS

BOILED "REDS"

GARLIC CHERRY TOMATOES

APPLES AND VERMONT CHEDDAR

BEVERAGE: LIGHT, FRUITY RED WINE

When I was growing up my mother used to say to me "Eat your liver, it's good for you." It's funny, I didn't like it much then, but now I do enjoy it occasionally.

I think the simplest preparation is the best. Bring water to the boil first and start cooking the potatoes. Then begin to brown the onions for the liver. Sauté cherry tomatoes in a skillet with olive oil, crushed garlic, and parsley. Throw in some chopped fresh basil, if it's that time of year. Next, quickly pan-fry the liver.

For dessert serve apples and a wedge of Vermont cheddar.

Mom's calf's liver and onions

In a large skillet heat 2 tablespoons butter and vegetable oil. Add onion and salt and pepper and cook slowly until golden brown. Set aside. Melt more butter, if necessary. Dredge liver in flour, shaking off excess. Add to skillet and cook for about 1 minute over high heat until browned. Turn and cook for about 1 more minute. Set aside on platter.

Add 1 tablespoon butter to skillet, cook until golden brown, add vinegar, and bring to the boil scraping up brown bits. Return liver and onions to pan and reheat with sauce.

3 tablespoons butter
1 tablespoon vegetable oil
1 onion, thinly sliced
salt and pepper to taste
¾ pound calf's liver, thinly sliced
flour
2 teaspoons red wine vinegar

Some cheese facts...

1. *Several cheeses that are commonly considered for dessert are Brie, Port Salut, Beaumont.*
2. *When making sauces, add cheese near the end of cooking time to prevent it from becoming stringy and leathery.*
3. *Strong cheeses are best supported by equally heavy wines, and delicate cheeses call for light wines that won't overpower them.*
4. *Cheese that has become hard and dry can be grated and placed in an airtight container and refrigerated for later use.*
5. *Cheeses such as cheddar, Swiss, mozzarella, and Brie can be frozen if well wrapped. They should be used as soon as possible after thawing.*

More on potatoes...

1. *Idaho and other russet potatoes are the best to select for baking, mashing, and frying.*
2. *New potatoes are best for boiling and steaming.*
3. *Buy similar-size potatoes to ensure even cooking times.*
4. *If potatoes are peeled and sliced ahead of time, let them stand in a bowl of aciduated water (1 tablespoon vinegar or 2 tablespoons lemon juice per quart of water) until ready to use.*

Wurst Night

MENU

▲▲▲▲▲   BRAISED SAUSAGES
AND ONIONS

•••••   SAUERKRAUT

○ ○ ○   BLACK BREAD AND
BUTTER

▮▯▮▯▮▯▮   RED GRAPES AND
OATMEAL COOKIES

∨ ∨ ∨   BEVERAGE:
BEER

There aren't too many instructions for this plan of attack. Prepare the sausages first and then warm the sauerkraut!
For dessert serve seedless red grapes and big oatmeal cookies.

BRAISED SAUSAGES AND ONIONS

Melt butter in a skillet. Add onion and sauté for 5 minutes, until golden. Set aside. Add sausages to skillet and brown for 3 or 4 minutes per side. Add onion, beer, and bay leaf, and bring to the boil. Reduce heat and simmer for 20 minutes, turning sausages occasionally.

2 tablespoons butter
1 onion, thinly sliced
1 pound pork sausage
    links, 1½ inches in
    diameter
12 ounces beer
1 bay leaf

ON SAUSAGES...

There are many different kinds of sausages to choose from, and with a little detective work, you can even find them nitrite-free.

The braised sausage dish here could be made with an assortment of sausages if you like. Some additional selections might be:

Bockwurst	*Breakfast sausage*
Bratwurst	*Saucisson*
Boudin Blanc	*Knackwurst*
Italian sausage	*Kielbasa*

Elegant Dinner Just for Two

MENU

ooooo **NORMANDY-STYLE PORK CHOPS**

≈≈≈≈≈ **BUTTERED BRUSSELS SPROUTS**

⁄⁄⁄⁄ **CARROT STICKS**

▲▲▲▲▲ **GINGERBREAD**

|ıı|ıı| **BEVERAGE: LIGHT, FRUITY RED WINE**

*B*ring water to the boil first for Brussels sprouts. While the pork chops are cooking, boil the Brussels sprouts for 10 to 15 minutes, or until tender. Drain and toss with butter, salt, and pepper. Cut up the carrots.

For dessert stop at the bakery for gingerbread squares. If you want to be really sinful, top with a dollop of whipped cream.

NORMANDY-STYLE PORK CHOPS

Sprinkle chops with salt and pepper. Heat oil in a large heavy skillet. Add chops and brown for about 5 minutes. Turn and brown other side for about 10 minutes. Push chops to the edge of pan. Add apple slices in one layer. Cook for about 10 minutes, turning the apples so they brown. Set aside chops and apples. Pour fat out of skillet. Add brandy and ginger. Bring to the boil, stirring to dissolve browned particles. Add chicken stock and boil until reduced to a saucelike consistency. Serve sauce over chops and apples.

2 loin pork chops, about 1 inch thick
salt and pepper to taste
2 tablespoons vegetable oil
1 apple, peeled, cored, and thickly sliced
2 tablespoons applejack or brandy
1 teaspoon ground ginger
¾ cup chicken stock

ON SAUTÉING...

1. Use an old-fashioned spatter lid to keep grease from spattering.
2. When sautéing several different things individually for a dish, use an oversize sauté pan and do all at once in different sections of the pan.
3. Use a bulb baster to remove excess grease from the skillet.
4. To prevent grease from splattering, sprinkle a little salt in the skillet before pan-frying hamburgers.
5. To prevent scorching when sautéing with butter, add some cooking oil to the butter.
6. Do not crowd the pan when sautéing or the food will actually steam.

COOKING THE PRESSURE COOKER WAY

MENU

BRAISED PORK CHOPS WITH SWEET POTATOES AND APPLES

GREEN BEANS

COOKIES

BEVERAGE: LIGHT, FRUITY RED WINE

When time is of the essence, plug in the pressure cooker! The new models cook succulent fancies, like these pork chops, in a snap. (You won't finish Moby Dick *while your soup simmers, but you'll cut the time you spent watching the water boil.)*

Cooking at 15 pounds of pressure (the average amount) cuts down on conventional cooking time by roughly two-thirds and seals in more nutrients.

Because this pork-chop recipe already includes a starch, the only other thing to prepare is the green beans. Serve your favorite cookies for dessert.

BRAISED PORK CHOPS WITH SWEET POTATOES AND APPLES

Melt 3 tablespoons butter in a cooker. Season pork chops with salt, pepper, and thyme and dredge lightly in flour, shaking off excess. Brown chops 1 to 2 minutes on each side. Add sweet potatoes and apples around chops, and dot chops with remaining 1 tablespoon butter. Close the lid and cook at low heat for 10 minutes, once 15 pounds of pressure has been reached. When cooking time is over, allow steam to escape, and lower pressure before removing lid.

4 tablespoons butter
4 thick pork chops, trimmed
salt and pepper to taste
1 teaspoon dried thyme
2 tablespoons flour
4 sweet potatoes, quartered
4 apples, peeled, cored, and quartered

PRESSURE-COOKING TIPS...

1. *Do not fill a pressure cooker more than two-thirds full when making soup.*

2. *Always be sure to exhaust the air in the cooker before capping the vent, as trapped air can cause uneven cooking. Allow steam to come out in a solid column before capping.*

3. *Cooking times begin from the moment correct pressure is reached.*

4. *The cover must not be removed until the steam is out of the cooker.*

5. *When foods require different cooking times, begin with the ingredients that require the most time. Always reduce pressure as directed in the manufacturer's manual before opening the lid to add foods with shorter cooking times.*

6. *This chart gives an idea of the time you can save by using a pressure cooker.*

FOOD	PRESSURE COOKER	NORMAL METHOD
Roast pork	30 minutes	2 hours
Coq au vin	30 minutes	1½ hours
Stuffed peppers	16 minutes	30–40 minutes
Carrots (¼ inch)	2–3 minutes	8–10 minutes

VEGETARIAN

Vegetable Feast

MENU

ᒃᒃᒃᒃᒃ EGGPLANT
ROLLATINI

▲▲▲▲▲ CAESAR SALAD
(SEE PAGE 248)

||●||●||●|| BREAD STICKS

✧✧✧✧✧ COFFEE ICE CREAM
WITH POWDERED
COFFEE BEANS

⁄⁄⁄⁄ BEVERAGE:
LIGHT, FRUITY
RED WINE

*F*or this menu the eggplant
rollatini is definitely the star,
so pop it in the oven before
assembling the ingredients for
the Caesar salad.
For dessert grind espresso
beans in a blender until
powdered. Use to garnish
coffee ice cream.

EGGPLANT ROLLATINI

Preheat oven to 350°. Grease a shallow baking dish. Heat 2 tablespoons olive oil in a large skillet and sauté eggplant on each side until softened and golden. Repeat with remaining oil and eggplant. Drain on paper towels.

In mixing bowl combine the cheeses, egg, salt and pepper, and parsley. Spread filling on each slice, roll up jelly-roll fashion, or fold in half like a turnover, and place seam side down in a baking dish. Pour some tomato sauce over top and bake for 20 minutes, or until tender.

¼ cup olive oil
1 pound large eggplant, cut into ¼-inch slices
6 ounces ricotta cheese
4 ounces mozzarella cheese, shredded
3 tablespoons grated Parmesan cheese
2 tablespoons beaten egg
salt and pepper to taste
2 tablespoons chopped fresh parsley
1½ cups store-bought meatless tomato sauce

ABOUT SALADS...

1. *Try coarsely chopped taco shells if you run out of croutons.*
2. *Store salad greens by washing, shaking off excess water, and storing in the refrigerator, wrapped in paper towels and a plastic bag.*
3. *Add longer life to fresh herbs by storing the stem ends in a glass of water and covering the top with plastic wrap.*
4. *Prepare a double batch of rice for dinner and use the extra rice the next day with leftover meat or poultry, vegetables, and herbs for a main dish salad.*

INDIAN SUMMER DINNER

MENU

ZUCCHINI FRITTATA

TOMATO SALAD WITH GARLIC CROUTONS

CRUSTY SOURDOUGH BREAD

RIPE PEARS WITH BLUE CHEESE AND WALNUTS

BEVERAGE: SPARKLING MINERAL WATER

Indian summer is the perfect time of the year to enjoy the last of summer's bounty. Zucchini, tomatoes, and basil are in great abundance and cheap to boot. Then, for dessert, usher in fall with wonderful fresh pears. While the frittata is cooking, slice the tomatoes and arrange on a plate. Top with coarse salt and freshly ground black pepper. Sprinkle with olive oil and some balsamic or red wine vinegar. Garnish with "ribbons" of fresh basil and croutons. Serve the pears with an interesting blue cheese, and walnuts in the shell for cracking. If you really want to go all out, finish with a wonderful glass of Port. This combination can't be beat.

ZUCCHINI FRITTATA

In a 10-inch skillet heat oil. Sauté onion and garlic for 5 minutes until softened. Add zucchini and sauté for 3 minutes more. Remove from heat.

In a bowl beat eggs and salt lightly. Add zucchini mixture and 6 tablespoons Parmesan.

Melt 1 tablespoon butter in same skillet. When hot, pour in egg mixture. Reduce heat to low and cook for about 20 minutes, or until eggs are set, without stirring.

Loosen edges of frittata and invert onto a plate. Melt remaining 1 tablespoon butter in skillet and slide frittata back into pan to cook on other side. Sprinkle with remaining 2 tablespoons Parmesan and red pepper. Cook for 5 minutes, or run under broiler briefly to brown top. Serve cut in wedges. Good hot or at room temperature. Serve leftovers the next day at an Indian summer picnic.

3 tablespoons olive oil
1 medium onion, thinly sliced
1 clove garlic, minced
2 cups grated unpeeled zucchini
6 eggs
½ teaspoon salt
½ cup grated Parmesan cheese
2 tablespoons butter
crushed dried hot red pepper flakes

ON EGGS...

1. *Press a thin layer of leftover cooked spaghetti on the bottom and sides of a greased quiche pan. Pour in quiche filling and*

bake as usual. Cut in wedges.

2. *Fold applesauce and a touch of cinnamon into an egg mixture for a different omelette.*

3. *Use your hand as a "strainer" to separate yolks from whites. Crack the eggs over a clean bowl into your hand. Separate your fingers slightly and allow the whites to fall into the bowl, leaving the yolk in your hand.*

4. *Use greased ovenproof custard cups for making poached eggs. Place the eggs in the cups in a pan filled with 1 inch of simmering water, covered. Serve in same cups.*

5. *Use a ricer or potato masher to chop hard-boiled eggs quickly.*

6. *If you have curdled an egg-based sauce, add a couple of ice cubes and whisk.*

7. *Pricking eggs with a pin keeps them from cracking.*

8. *If you forget whether a stored egg is hard-boiled, spin it on the counter. Cooked eggs spin smoothly; uncooked ones wobble.*

9. *Freeze extra egg whites in plastic containers, marking with the number of whites. Run the container under warm water to hasten thawing. Use when making meringues, macaroons, floating island, etc.*

POTATOES —FAST AND FILLING

MENU

TWICE-BAKED POTATOES   ✓✓✓✓

GREEN SALAD   ～～～

TIPSY ORANGES   ▨▨▨

BEVERAGE: ICED TEA COOLER   ○ ○ ○

A baked potato is one of the more foolproof foods to prepare in the microwave. We are elevating the plain potato to new heights by actually turning it into a healthy and nutritious dinner. Lean in calories (a 5-ounce potato has just 100) and loaded with energy-boosting complex carbohydrates, the potato is a near-perfect food—and dressed up, it's a meal in itself. By eliminating the ham in the recipe, it is perfect for the vegetarian in your family. Serve your twice-baked potato with a green salad, including some black olives, luscious ripe red tomatoes from the last of the season's harvest, and some fresh chopped basil. Don't forget to pass the extra filling with the potatoes. For the iced tea cooler, combine iced tea with equal parts club soda or ginger ale for a refreshing change. For dessert, peel two seedless oranges, slice thinly, and let marinate in Grand Marnier during dinner.

TWICE-BAKED POTATOES

2 large potatoes
5 ounces frozen broccoli
 spears
¼ cup heavy cream or
 milk
½ cup cottage cheese
¼ cup coarsely chopped
 ham (optional)
2 tablespoons grated
 Gruyère or Swiss
 cheese
½ teaspoon salt
pinch black pepper
pinch grated nutmeg

Pierce potatoes twice with a fork to allow excess steam to escape. Place 1 inch apart on paper towel on shelf of microwave oven. Cook on HIGH for 5½ to 6½ minutes, turning and rearranging once. Potatoes will still feel slightly firm when done; wrap each in aluminum foil and set aside to soften for 5 minutes.

Place broccoli in a 1-quart casserole, covered. Microwave on HIGH for 4 to 5 minutes, or until tender, rearranging once. Let stand, covered, for 1 to 2 minutes. Chop coarsely.

Slice top from each potato. With teaspoon, remove center of potato, leaving potato shell intact, and place potato flesh in mixing bowl. Mash potato flesh with broccoli, cream or milk, cottage cheese, ham, 1 tablespoon grated cheese, salt, pepper, and nutmeg. Spoon stuffing into reserved shells. Sprinkle remaining 1 tablespoon cheese on top. (Note: any extra filling may be baked separately in a microwavable dish.) Arrange potatoes on microwavable plate and cook on MEDIUM-HIGH for 2 minutes, or until cheese melts.

To prepare potatoes in a conventional oven, preheat oven to 375°. Add potatoes and bake for 45 minutes to 1 hour, or until soft. While baking, cook frozen broccoli according to package directions. Make filling and assemble potatoes as described above. Arrange stuffed potatoes on a cookie sheet and bake in a preheated 425° oven until cheese melts.

Microwave Hot Spot Test...

Arrange trimmed bread slices on the floor of the oven. Set on HIGH and watch how the bread browns. This will show where the oven is hottest.

How to Test Utensils for Microwave Use...

Place 1 cup cool water in a Pyrex measuring cup in the microwave, next to the dish you are testing. Heat on HIGH for 1 minute. If the dish is warm, it is absorbing microwave energy and should not be used in the microwave.

SUPERMARKET STIR-FRY

MENU

▲▲▲▲▲▲ VEGETABLE STIR-FRY

ℓℓℓℓℓℓ RICE WITH CHOPPED
SCALLIONS

▪▪▪▪▪▪ LEMON ICE AND
ALMOND COOKIES

∘∘∘∘∘∘ BEVERAGE:
GREEN TEA

Supermarkets have changed quite a lot. Now, more often than not, the produce department of your local supermarket will offer assorted vegetables all cut up for you. The market's idea is for you to take the produce home in the form of a salad. Our idea is for you to take it home, maybe add some sautéed cubed chicken, and stir-fry it for dinner. With all the chopping done, actual cooking time is minimal. Begin by preparing the rice first and 5 minutes before it is done, start to stir-fry the vegetables. Note: *You may vary your assortment of vegetables according to what's at the supermarket salad bar or to your taste. For a refreshing dessert try lemon ice and store-bought almond cookies.*

VEGETABLE STIR-FRY

Heat the vegetable oil in a wok or large skillet over high heat. Add green onions and carrots and stir-fry for 30 seconds. Add remaining vegetables and stir-fry for 2 minutes longer. Add salt, sugar, ginger, soy sauce, and sesame oil. Stir, cook for 30 seconds, and serve.

- 3 tablespoons vegetable oil
- 4 green onions, sliced
- 2 small carrots cut into sticks
- 1 head of broccoli, cut into florets
- 1 can (8 ounces) bamboo shoots, sliced
- 4 ounces snow peas
- 4 ounces mushrooms, sliced
- 2 medium zucchini, cut into sticks
- ½ cup bean sprouts
- ½ teaspoon salt
- ½ teaspoon sugar
- ½ teaspoon minced fresh ginger
- 1 tablespoon soy sauce
- 1 tablespoon sesame oil

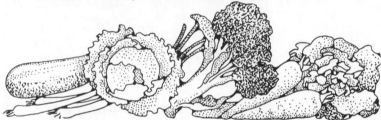

ON VEGETABLES...

1. *Freeze leftover vegetables when you have at least 2 cups and save for soup. Thaw and puree in food processor. Add chicken or beef stock and some heavy cream until you have the desired consistency. Season with salt and pepper.*
2. *When you need a small amount of grated onion, place the onion in a garlic press.*
3. *Add a few tablespoons of minced chutney to a cup of plain yogurt to make a dip for raw vegetables.*
4. *Keep white vegetables white by adding lemon juice to the cooking water.*

VEGETARIAN NIGHT

MENU

•••••• CONSOMMÉ

⬝⬝⬝⬝⬝ ARTICHOKE
SQUARES

▪▪▪▪▪▪ MIXED SALAD

◆◆◆◆◆ FRESH APRICOTS

⁄⁄⁄⁄⁄ BEVERAGE:
SPARKLING
WATER
WITH LIME

This artichoke dish from Joni Muskovitz, a high-school friend, makes more than 2 can eat for dinner. Since this dish is quite versatile, serve it for dinner one night and have leftovers the next day, room temperature, at a picnic, or cut into small squares to reheat and serve as an hors d'oeuvre. Even better yet, it can be frozen and reheats beautifully. Serve with consommé and a mixed salad to round out your meal. Serve fresh apricots, when in season, for dessert—or good-quality dried apricots soaked in cognac to soften.

ARTICHOKE SQUARES

Preheat oven to 350°. Grease a 9″-x-13″ pan. Drain off and discard juice from one jar of artichokes. Combine all remaining ingredients in a large bowl.

Pour mixture into the pan and spread evenly in a thin layer. Bake for 30 minutes. Cut in squares and serve.

2 6-ounce jars marinated artichoke hearts
½ cup chopped onion
1 clove garlic, minced
4 eggs, beaten
¼ cup bread crumbs
¼ teaspoon salt
1 teaspoon dried oregano
black pepper to taste
4 drops Tabasco sauce
½ pound sharp cheddar cheese, shredded
3 tablespoons minced fresh parsley

ON RIPENING, THE PAPER BAG WAY...

When you don't have time to make a lot of trips to the supermarket and can't always buy ripe produce for the day you want to use it, ripen the produce yourself at home. Put it inside a brown paper bag, close the bag, and punch one little hole in it with the tip of a knife. Let sit on the kitchen counter until the fruit is ripe. Check frequently. It usually takes 3 days to ripen pears and 1 to 2 days to ripen peaches, nectarines, or apricots.

TREE-TRIMMING SUPPER

M E N U

CHEESE FONDUE

FRENCH BREAD

APPLE AND CELERY CHUNKS

ASSORTED SALAMIS

CHRISTMAS COOKIES

BEVERAGE:
HOT AND SPICY
BLOODY MARYS

This tree-trimming supper is designed for 2, you and a favorite someone to share it with. If you end up inviting a bigger crowd, just double or triple the recipe and add more "go-withs."

Lew Paper's recipe for Cheese Fondue is an old favorite and can be kept warm over a can of Sterno while you take a minute to add another ornament to the tree. Serve chunks of French bread for dipping and, on a lighter note, pieces of apple and celery.

Make your favorite recipe for Bloody Marys up to the point of adding vodka. Heat in a saucepan and add vodka before serving. Serve in heatproof mugs. For dessert buy or bake your favorite sugar-butter holiday cookies.

CHEESE FONDUE

Rub fondue pot or an earthenware casserole with cut side of garlic clove. Add wine to pot and heat on stove. When wine is hot, but not boiling, add lemon juice. Turn heat to low and slowly add cheeses, stirring constantly. It will look lumpy but will smooth out later. Stir and cook until smooth. Add oregano, garlic powder, Tabasco, and Worcestershire. Add cornstarch-wine mixture to pot and stir just until it bubbles and thickens. Place casserole over a can of Sterno with a slow flame. Serve with chunks of French bread, celery, and apples.

1 clove garlic, peeled and halved
1 cup dry white wine
1½ teaspoons lemon juice
6 ounces Gruyère cheese, grated
6 ounces Emmenthaler cheese, grated
pinch dried oregano
pinch garlic powder
3 drops Tabasco sauce
⅛ teaspoon Worcestershire sauce
1 tablespoon cornstarch mixed with 1 tablespoon dry white wine

ON COOKING WITH WINE...

Don't use any old wine to cook with. The alcohol is what evaporates during cooking, not the flavor. You don't need to choose one of your best expensive wines, but don't select the worst either! If you wouldn't drink it yourself—it is not good enough for the pot.

SOUPS, SANDWICHES, AND SALADS

SOUP AND SANDWICH SUPPER

MENU

GAZPACHO

TUNA NIÇOISE SANDWICH

LIME ICE

BEVERAGE: DOUBLE ICED TEA

This menu is perfect for a hot summer evening. Appetites seem to decrease when the temperature goes up, but you shouldn't just skip dinner. When produce is at its peak, it is the perfect time to make a no-cook soup such as gazpacho. While the soup is chilling in the refrigerator, assemble your sandwich. When making tuna niçoise be sure to include some of the following: tuna, green beans, black olives, anchovies, red onion, vinaigrette dressing, tomatoes, and hard-boiled eggs. Slice the baguette lengthwise and brush with some of the vinaigrette dressing. Arrange the salad open-face on top of the baguette. Other sandwich combinations are endless. Double iced tea is the way to prevent your tea from being diluted by melting ice cubes. Freeze some iced tea in ice cube trays and add that to your glass of iced tea. Serve a refreshing lime ice for dessert.

Gazpacho

In a bowl mash together garlic and salt. Stir in oil to form a paste. Add the remaining ingredients. Stir to combine. Refrigerate until serving time. Serve in chilled soup bowls garnished with additional chopped green peppers and onions.

½ teaspoon minced garlic
¼ teaspoon salt
2 tablespoons olive oil
2¼ cups tomatoes, chopped (about 1½ pounds)
¼ cup minced green bell pepper, plus extra for garnish
1 cucumber, peeled and chopped
¼ cup minced onion, plus extra for garnish
1 cup tomato juice, chilled
1½ tablespoons red wine vinegar
dash cayenne pepper
3 tablespoons chopped fresh dill
black pepper to taste

ON ICED TEA...

1. Save leftover fruit juice and mix into a pitcher of iced tea for extra zip.
2. Stir lemon zest into a jar of granulated sugar and cover. After sugar has absorbed lemon flavor, use sugar in tea.
3. Try using more unusual teas to make iced tea for a change, such as Red Zinger.

ON FRESH TUNA VERSUS CANNED...

The next time you grill tuna for dinner, make extra and use in tuna niçoise the next day. It gives a whole new dimension to tuna salad!

ANOTHER SOUP AND SANDWICH SUPPER

MENU

BANANA BISQUE WITH CINNAMON CROUTONS

CURRIED CHICKEN SALAD IN BRIOCHE

CRUDITÉS

FRESH PINEAPPLE WITH RUM SPLASH

BEVERAGE: SPARKLING MINERAL WATER WITH A WEDGE OF LIME

*T*his refreshing banana bisque can be made in a flash and set in the freezer to chill while you make your sandwich. Since the banana bisque has an island flavor, stop on your way home at your favorite take-out spot for some curried chicken salad to serve with the bisque. Serve either in a hollowed out brioche or in a pineapple boat. For a refreshing dessert serve sliced fresh pineapple sprinkled with sugar and rum to taste.

Banana Bisque with Cinnamon Croutons

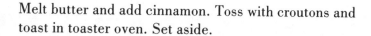

1 tablespoon butter
⅛ teaspoon ground
    cinnamon
¼ cup unseasoned
    croutons
2 cups milk
1–2 bananas (depending
    on thickness you
    want of bisque)
1 tablespoon mango
    chutney
2 tablespoons dark rum

Melt butter and add cinnamon. Toss with croutons and toast in toaster oven. Set aside.

In food processor or blender, puree milk, bananas, chutney, and rum. Pour into chilled soup bowls or mugs and garnish with croutons.

Prepare this as close to serving time as possible.

CURRIED CHICKEN SALAD

½ cup mayonnaise
¼ cup sour cream
1 tablespoon curry powder
1 tablespoon chutney
salt and pepper, to taste

2 cups cooked chicken,
   cut in ¼-inch strips
1 tablespoon raisins
¼ cup apples, chopped
2 tablespoons peanuts

In a bowl combine mayonnaise, sour cream, curry powder, chutney, salt and pepper. Stir in chicken, raisins, apples and peanuts. Adjust seasonings to taste.

ON POACHING CHICKEN BREASTS...

I like to poach chicken breasts instead of whole chickens in order to get quick-cooked chicken to use in dishes such as chicken potpie, chicken hash, and chicken salad.

Arrange ¾ pound boneless, skinless chicken breasts in saucepan. Add 1 cup water, salt to taste, 2 slices onion, pinch dried thyme, 1 bay leaf, and a sprig parsley. Bring to the boil, cover, and simmer for 5 minutes. Remove from heat and let stand in broth until ready to use. Makes 2 cups.

SANDWICH SUPPER

MENU

SMOKED CHICKEN
AND ROQUEFORT
SANDWICH

CARROT AND CELERY
STICKS

HONEY-RICOTTA
PEACHES

BEVERAGE:
LEMONADE

*P*reparation for this menu begins with the dessert. In a bowl whisk ⅔ cup ricotta cheese until smooth. Slice 2 peaches in half, remove the pits, and fill centers with ricotta. Drizzle honey to taste over all and crumble an amaretti cookie on top. Cut the carrots and celery into sticks and prepare the sandwiches.

SMOKED CHICKEN AND ROQUEFORT SANDWICH

Spread bread with your favorite mustard. Arrange lettuce, then chicken, and top with Roquefort. Serve open-face.

2 slices white or
    pumpernickel
    bread
mustard
curly lettuce
4 ounces smoked
    chicken, thinly
    sliced
4 ounces Roquefort,
    crumbled

OTHER SANDWICH COMBOS...

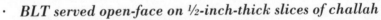

- *BLT served open-face on ½-inch-thick slices of challah*
- *lobster club sandwich on sliced brioche*
- *Gorgonzola cheese and salami on black bread*
- *prosciutto, provolone, radicchio, and sliced tomatoes with vinaigrette on peasant bread*
- *smoked turkey, Vermont cheddar, lettuce, tomato, and mayonnaise on pumpernickel*

SUPPER FOR A HOT NIGHT

MENU

○○○○○ WARM CHINESE CHICKEN SALAD

▮▯▮▯▮▯▮▯▮ DINNER ROLLS

▼▼▼▼▼ DECADENT CHOCOLATE-DIPPED CLEMENTINES

▪▪▪▪▪ BEVERAGE: BEER

This menu begins with the preparation of dessert. Peel and section clementines (or oranges) and set aside. Melt 3 ounces semisweet chocolate. Keep warm over simmering water.

Pop the rolls in the oven and then prepare the chicken salad.

For dessert pour the melted chocolate into a small ramekin or bowl and arrange clementines on a plate. Using your fingers, dip the clementines into as much chocolate as your heart desires!

Warm Chinese Chicken Salad

In food processor fitted with a steel blade puree ¼ cup peanut oil, sesame oil, ginger, garlic, vinegar or sherry, and soy sauce.

Heat 1 tablespoon peanut oil in a large skillet. Add chicken and sauté quickly until it loses its pink color. Set aside. Pour oil out of skillet and add dressing to skillet. When hot, add mushrooms. Stir-fry for 1 minute. Add snow peas, chicken, and celery. Stir-fry for 2 minutes to warm.

Arrange bean sprouts on plates and top with warm chicken mixture. Sprinkle sesame seeds on top.

DRESSING:

¼ cup plus 1 tablespoon
    peanut oil
1 tablespoon sesame oil
1 tablespoon minced
    ginger
1 clove garlic, minced
2 tablespoons rice
    vinegar or dry
    sherry
1 tablespoon soy sauce

¾ pound chicken
    breasts, boneless
    and skinless, cut
    into strands ¼" x 2"
    long
½ cup canned straw
    mushrooms
    (optional)
3 ounces snow peas,
    julienned
½ cup thinly sliced
    celery
½ pound bean sprouts
1 tablespoon toasted
    sesame seeds

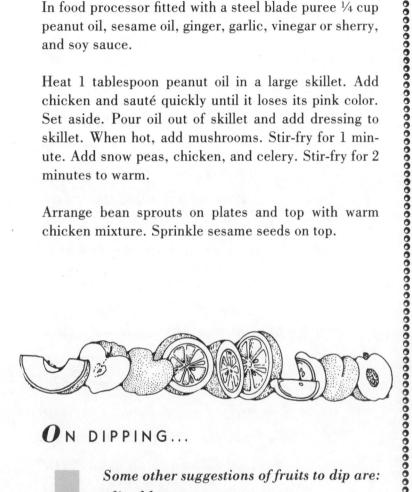

On Dipping...

Some other suggestions of fruits to dip are:
- · *sliced bananas*
- · *orange sections*
- · *strawberries*
- · *sliced pears*
- · *raspberries*
- · *sliced figs*
- · *tangerine sections*

CARIBBEAN FLAVOR

MENU

▲▲▲▲▲▲ CURRIED SHRIMP SALAD

○ ○ ○ ○ SLICED AVOCADO

▪▪▪▪▪▪ DINNER ROLLS

〰〰 ISLAND FRUIT PLATTER

○○○○○○ BEVERAGE: RUM PUNCH

*O*n a recent trip to the Caribbean, I tasted a wonderful, easy-to-prepare curried shrimp salad. The recipe comes from Jumby Bay Resort in Antigua. It was a pleasant surprise to find how simple it was to make. In Antigua it was made with tiny cooked shrimp, but you can substitute larger shrimp, cut in half. Frozen cooked shrimp from the supermarket can be kept on hand to avoid an extra shopping trip. Add some sliced avocado and dinner rolls for a thoroughly satisfying dinner. No visit to the Caribbean is complete without a rum punch to drink .

For dessert serve a fresh fruit platter made up of an assortment of the following: banana, pineapple, orange, grapefruit, mango, and papaya. Sprinkle each serving with a little lime juice and dark rum.

CURRIED SHRIMP SALAD

In a bowl combine mayonnaise, curry powder, and lemon juice. Add shrimp, raisins, green onions, and season with salt and pepper. Garnish with coconut and serve on a bed of Bibb lettuce.

- ½ cup mayonnaise
- 2 teaspoons curry powder
- ½ teaspoon lemon juice
- 1½ pounds cooked shrimp
- 3 tablespoons raisins
- 3 green onions, thinly sliced
- salt and pepper to taste
- shredded coconut (optional)
- Bibb lettuce

JUMBY'S RUM PUNCH

Here is Jumby Bay's secret recipe!

3 tablespoons Antiguan rum
2 tablespoons sugar syrup
2 tablespoons lime juice

2–3 dashes angostura bitters
grated nutmeg

Fill a short tumbler with ice. Add rum, sugar syrup, lime juice, and bitters; stir. Sprinkle a pinch nutmeg on top. *Serves 1.*

NOTE : *Sugar syrup can be made ahead and stored indefinitely to be used in other drinks. In a saucepan combine 1½ cups sugar and ½ cup cold water. Bring to the boil and boil for 3 minutes. Cool and store in screw-top jar in refrigerator.*

ONE MORE TIME

MENU

MASTER CHEF
SALAD

CROISSANTS

ASSORTED
HOLIDAY
PIES AND
DESSERTS

BEVERAGE:
CRANGRAPE
FIZZ

This Master Chef Salad is good anytime, but it's perfect for using up Thanksgiving or Christmas leftover turkey, roast beef, and/or ham. Serve the salad with store-bought croissants, leftover muffins, or popovers warmed in the oven. To make the Crangrape Fizz pour into an ice-filled glass ½ cup grapefruit juice, ¼ cup cranberry juice, and top off with club soda. Stir and serve. Serves 1. For dessert it is time to go back to the pantry to savor the last of your holiday pies and desserts.

Master chef salad

In a large bowl combine all salad ingredients, except blue cheese. In a small jar with a tight-fitting lid combine vinaigrette ingredients and shake well. Pour over salad and toss; sprinkle blue cheese on top.

2 cups torn romaine or
  leaf lettuce pieces
1 avocado, peeled and
  diced
2 cups cubed turkey or
  other leftover meat
6 slices bacon, cooked
  crisply and
  crumbled
1 large tomato, diced
1 large cucumber,
  peeled and diced
2 ounces blue cheese,
  crumbled

VINAIGRETTE:

2 tablespoons red wine
  vinegar
6 tablespoons olive oil
1 teaspoon Dijon
  mustard
salt and pepper to taste

On microwaving bacon...

Line a microwave roasting rack or paper plate with 2 layers of paper towels. Arrange 6 strips of bacon on top and cover with 2 layers of paper towels. Heat on HIGH for 3½ to 4 minutes.

THE NO-LETTUCE SALAD DINNER

MENU

ANTIPASTO
SALAD

ITALIAN
FLATBREAD

BLACKBERRIES
'N' YOGURT

BEVERAGE:
ICED TEA

This Antipasto Salad is a filling main course when served with Italian flatbread. Make the salad first and set aside to blend the flavors while you catch up on your mail. This dinner is so easy, there's nothing for you to do! For dessert fold 1 cup blackberries (you can also use strawberries, blueberries, or raspberries) into 2 containers of vanilla yogurt.

ANTIPASTO SALAD

In a screw-top jar combine dressing ingredients.

In bottom of a glass bowl arrange provolone slices, overlapping, and sprinkle cheese cubes on top. Sprinkle on some basil. Pour some dressing over the cheese. Arrange salami slices and tomato on top of that. Pour dressing on and top with remaining basil. Set aside for flavors to blend.

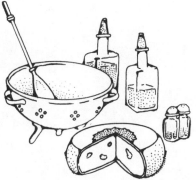

DRESSING:

2 tablespoons red wine
    vinegar
4 tablespoons olive oil
salt and pepper to taste
1 tablespoon thinly
    sliced green onions

1½ ounces provolone,
    thinly sliced
3 ounces Swiss cheese,
    cut into ½-inch
    cubes
¼ cup coarsely chopped
    basil leaves
3 ounces Genoa salami,
    thinly sliced
1 tomato, thinly sliced

ON BERRIES...

1. *To prevent spoilage, don't wash berries until ready to use.*
2. *Remove plastic wrapping from berry boxes and rewrap in wax paper to keep fresh.*
3. *To prevent bruising ripe fruit, the fruit should be cold, not room temperature, when it is washed.*

PIZZA AND PASTA

PIZZA PRONTO

MENU

"HAM AND CHEESE" PIZZA

GREEN SALAD

FRESH FRUIT

ESPRESSO

BEVERAGE: LIGHT, FRUITY RED WINE

*E*ven if you can't flip and twirl the pizza dough, don't be afraid to make it. You can use a rolling pin to stretch it out or just pat with your fingertips onto a cookie sheet. Better yet, you don't even have to make the dough yourself, unless, of course, you are looking for a weekend project for the family. Pizza (or bread) dough is now available in the freezer case or refrigerator compartment at the supermarket.

Pizza is no longer just tomato sauce and one kind of cheese. Varieties are endless and can be as healthy and nutritious as the toppings you select. So let yourself go and have family members "customize" their own individual pizzas. For dessert serve fresh fruit and espresso.

"HAM AND CHEESE" PIZZA

Preheat oven to 450°. Sauté pepper and garlic in 1 tablespoon olive oil until soft. Roll or pat pizza into two 9-inch circles and place on cookie sheet. Brush top of dough with remaining 1 tablespoon olive oil and sprinkle with half of basil or thyme. Arrange mozzarella on top. Place tomatoes, overlapping, ham, green onions, peppers, and garlic decoratively on top. Sprinkle with goat cheese and top with remaining herbs.

Bake on middle and lower racks of oven (reversing part way through if using 2 cookie sheets). Otherwise, bake on lowest shelf for approximately 20 minutes, or until crust is golden brown.

1 red bell pepper, minced
3 cloves garlic, minced
2 tablespoons olive oil
¾ pound pizza dough, fresh or frozen
3 tablespoons chopped fresh basil or thyme
¾ pound mozzarella, grated
6 plum tomatoes, sliced
3 ounces ham, julienned
1 bunch green onions, thinly sliced (white part only)
3 ounces goat cheese, crumbled

SOME PIZZA VARIATIONS...

Any of these combinations can be layered on halved French bread and heated in a 350° oven:

· *tomato sauce, artichoke hearts, thyme, mozzarella and Romano cheeses*

- *sautéed onions and garlic, salt and pepper, mixed herbs, and Parmesan*
- *sautéed spinach, onion, garlic, salt and pepper, topped with olives and slivers of mozzarella*
- *blanched asparagus, ham, thyme, and goat cheese.*

OMEMADE PIZZA DOUGH ∨∨∨∨∨∨∨∨∨∨∨∨ ∨∨∨

1 package dry yeast	½ teaspoon salt
1¼ cups warm water	2 tablespoons olive oil
1 teaspoon sugar	4 cups unbleached flour

In a small bowl sprinkle yeast over ¼ cup warm water. Add ½ teaspoon sugar and stir to combine. Set aside.

Place remaining 1 cup warm water in a large mixing bowl. Add salt and remaining ½ teaspoon sugar. Stir to dissolve. Add oil and gradually stir in flour. Add yeast mixture. Stir to combine.

On a lightly floured board, knead dough for 5 minutes, or until smooth. Place in a greased clean mixing bowl and set aside, covered with a damp cloth, in a warm place for 1 hour. *Makes four 9-inch pizzas.*

*T*he *preparation of this menu starts at the end and finishes at the beginning! First scoop out melon balls, sprinkle lemon juice on them, and garnish with mint. Set aside in the refrigerator.*
Slice 2 zucchini and 2 carrots thinly while preparing the cream sauce for the casserole. While the casserole is baking in the oven, stir-fry the vegetables. Melt 2 tablespoons butter in a skillet, add the zucchini, carrots, and salt and pepper to taste. Stir-fry for 3 minutes. Add 3 tablespoons chicken stock or water, cover, and cook for a few minutes more, until the vegetables are tender.

CASSEROLE SUPPER

MENU

GREEN NOODLE CASSEROLE WITH PROSCIUTTO

ZUCCHINI-CARROT TOSS

WHOLE-WHEAT ITALIAN BREAD

CITRUS MELON BALLS WITH MINT

BEVERAGE: DRY, LIGHT-BODIED WHITE WINE

GREEN NOODLE CASSEROLE WITH PROSCIUTTO

8 tablespoons butter
¼ cup flour
½ teaspoon salt
⅛ teaspoon black
  pepper
2 cups hot milk
½ cup heavy cream
6 ounces spinach
  fettuccine
¼ pound prosciutto or
  other ham, thinly
  sliced
¼ cup grated Parmesan
  cheese

Bring a large pot of salted water to the boil.

Melt 4 tablespoons butter in a saucepan. Add flour and cook, stirring, for 2 minutes. Add salt, pepper, and milk and cook, stirring until sauce is smooth and thickened. Cook over low heat for 5 minutes. Stir in cream.

Preheat oven to 350°. Grease a shallow baking dish. While sauce is cooking, boil fettuccine for 8 minutes. Drain and put in baking dish. Toss with 2 tablespoons butter and cream sauce. Arrange ham slices overlapping on top. Sprinkle on Parmesan and dot with remaining 2 tablespoons butter. Bake for 10 minutes.

ON CASSEROLES...

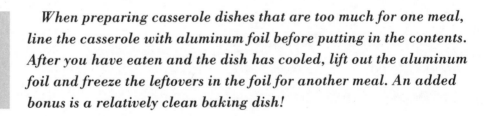

When preparing casserole dishes that are too much for one meal, line the casserole with aluminum foil before putting in the contents. After you have eaten and the dish has cooled, lift out the aluminum foil and freeze the leftovers in the foil for another meal. An added bonus is a relatively clean baking dish!

M E N U

TOMATO PASTA

GREEN SALAD

GARLIC TOASTS

GRAPEFRUIT
SECTIONS WITH
COINTREAU

BEVERAGE:
LIGHT, FRUITY RED
WINE

Y*ou're probably thinking tomato pasta, haricots verts, sun-dried tomatoes—what is she, crazy? Especially for a weeknight dinner. This is the luxury version. It can also be prepared with dried egg fettuccine, julienned green beans, and sun-dried tomatoes. The fettuccine and tomatoes should be staple items on your pantry shelf. This pasta dish is also a wonderful first course when served in small portions. Bring a pot of water to the boil first and start making the sauce. Slice French bread into ½-inch-thick pieces. Rub with olive oil and a peeled clove of* *garlic. Bake in a 375° oven until browned, turning once. Assemble the salad. For dessert section a grapefruit and sprinkle with Cointreau.*

Tomato Pasta

½ cup heavy cream
4 ounces goat cheese, crumbled
3 tablespoons olive oil
2 cloves garlic, minced
½ pound haricots verts, (or "regular" green beans), blanched
3 sun-dried tomatoes, julienned
3 tablespoons minced fresh parsley
10 ounces fresh tomato fettuccine
salt and pepper to taste

Bring a large pot of salted water to the boil.

In a saucepan heat heavy cream with 2 ounces goat cheese. Cook on moderate heat until mixture is creamy.

In a large skillet heat olive oil and add garlic, green beans, sun-dried tomatoes, and parsley. Cook briefly to combine flavors.

Cook pasta in boiling salted water. Drain, and add to skillet with vegetables. Add remaining 2 ounces cheese. Pour on warm cream mixture and toss to combine with salt and pepper.

On Cooking Fresh Pasta...

Fresh pasta is perishable and should be refrigerated. If not served the same day, freeze in plastic bags.

Bring 4 quarts of salted water to the boil for each pound of pasta—9 ounces of fresh pasta is enough for 2 main-course servings. Bring water to a full rolling boil before adding pasta. Slowly add pasta and stir once with a wooden spoon. Time is more crucial with fresh pasta than with dried because it cooks so quickly.

NAME	COOKING TIME
Angel hair	45–60 seconds
Linguine	1–1½ minutes
Fettuccine	2–2½ minutes

The first time I made this dish I used a wonderful garlic-and-parsley fresh pasta, but it would be equally good with egg fettuccine. Begin preparing the sauce and then assemble the Italian bread: In a bowl mash together softened butter and whatever chopped herbs you have on hand. Slice the bread ¼ inch thick, bake on a cookie sheet at 350° for 6 minutes. Turn the toasts over, spread with butter, and sprinkle Parmesan on top. Bake for 6 minutes more. For dessert serve espresso and biscotti (may be bought in supermarkets, in box or tin) for dipping.

RED, WHITE, AND GREEN DINNER

MENU

PASTA WITH SPINACH SAUCE ▲▲▲▲▲

SLICED TOMATOES ■ ■ ■ ■ ■

WHOLE-WHEAT ITALIAN BREAD WITH HERB BUTTER ○ ○ ○

BISCOTTI AND ESPRESSO + + + + + +

BEVERAGE: LIGHT, FRUITY RED WINE ▮▮▮▮▮▮▮

Pasta with Spinach Sauce

2 tablespoons olive oil
½ tin or 5 anchovy
    fillets, minced
1 clove garlic, minced
4 ounces fresh spinach,
    stemmed and
    coarsely chopped
1 bunch arugula
1 cup heavy cream
¾ cup chicken stock
black pepper to taste
pinch cayenne pepper
½ cup grated Parmesan
    cheese
½ pound fettuccine

Bring a pot of salted water to the boil for pasta.

In a skillet heat olive oil. Add anchovies and garlic. Sauté for 3 minutes, being careful not to brown garlic. Add spinach and arugula and cook until wilted. Add cream, stock, and peppers. Bring almost to boiling and reduce heat to simmering. (When sauce is simmering, add pasta to pot of boiling water and cook until al dente.) Cook sauce until it begins to thicken. Add Parmesan to sauce and stir to combine just before tossing with pasta.

Other Pasta Main Courses...

1. *Heat with homemade or canned chili.*
2. *Toss with Gorgonzola cream sauce and walnuts.*
3. *Toss with reduced heavy cream and a handful of chopped fresh herbs.*
4. *Serve with stir-fried beef and vegetables.*
5. *Toss with olive oil, sun-dried tomatoes, and crumbled goat cheese.*
6. *Serve with tomato sauce, marinated artichoke hearts, and Parmesan cheese.*
7. *If you're lucky enough to have leftover osso bucco, take shanks out of sauce, remove meat from the bones and cube. Toss with the sauce and pasta.*

On Tomatoes...

1. *To ripen tomatoes at home, keep them in a brown paper bag at room temperature with an apple. When ripe, refrigerate.*
2. *The easiest way to chop canned tomatoes is with kitchen shears right in the can itself.*

CORN TORTILLA WITH CRABMEAT AND GUACAMOLE

(RECIPE ON PAGE 164)

CHICKEN BREASTS WITH TWO MUSTARDS

(RECIPE ON PAGE 60)

Gazpacho and Tuna Niçoise Sandwich

(RECIPE ON PAGE 105)   (RECIPE ON PAGE 104)

SALMON HASH
(RECIPE ON PAGE 36)

TWICE-BAKED POTATO

(RECIPE ON PAGE 96)

ou will have good luck
your personal affairs.

GOURMET
TO GO:
ASSORTED
DIM SUM

SAUCES: SALSA,
TOMATO, AND
PESTO ◢
(RECIPES ON PAGES 136,
AND 137)

SHRIMP CREOLE ❤
(RECIPE ON PAGE 49)

SCALLOP AND PEPPER BROCHETTES

(RECIPE ON PAGE 173)

*M*ASTER CHEF SALAD

(RECIPE ON PAGE 117)

ZUCCHINI FRITTATA

(RECIPE ON PAGE 93)

STIR-FRIED SHRIMP WITH VEGETABLES

(RECIPE ON PAGE 161)

BRAISED PORK CHOPS WITH SWEET POTATOES AND APPLES

(RECIPE ON PAGE 89)

*H*AM AND CHEESE PIZZA

(RECIPE ON PAGE 121)

TURKEY CROUSTADES

(RECIPE ON PAGE 66)

CHEESE FONDUE

(RECIPE ON PAGE 103)

SPAGHETTI DINNER

MENU

SPAGHETTI WITH
TOMATO SAUCE ▪▪▪▪▪

OVEN-FRIED
EGGPLANT ○ ○ ○

SESAME
BREADSTICKS

MACAROONS AND
FRESH PINEAPPLE

BEVERAGE:
LIGHT, FRUITY RED
WINE ◆◆◆◆◆

*F*or a
*change, this menu gives
the recipe for the "go-with"
instead of the main course.
Start to boil the water for
spaghetti and then assemble
the eggplant. Serve the
spaghetti with your favorite
tomato sauce.
For dessert serve sliced fresh
pineapple with macaroons.*

OVEN-FRIED EGGPLANT

½ cup bread crumbs
¼ cup grated Parmesan
    cheese
salt and pepper to taste
1 teaspoon dried
    oregano
1 medium eggplant,
    peeled and sliced
    into 1″-x-4″ strips
¼ cup olive oil

Preheat oven to 375°. Line baking sheet with aluminum foil. In a large plastic bag combine bread crumbs, Parmesan, salt and pepper, and oregano. Coat eggplant with olive oil and toss in bag of bread-crumb mixture.

Place strips on baking sheet and bake for 20 minutes, or until crisp.

ON BREADING...

Instead of putting flour or bread crumbs in a shallow dish, save on cleanup time by using a disposable plastic bag or wax paper to "dip into."

A TASTE

OF

ITALY

MENU

**SPAGHETTI WITH
CLAM SAUCE**

**GREEN SALAD WITH
RED ONION RINGS**

**CRUSTY ITALIAN
BREAD**

**CITRUS MELON
BALLS WITH MINT**

**BEVERAGE:
DRY, LIGHT-BODIED
WHITE WINE**

*F*irst scoop
out the melon balls,
sprinkle with lime juice, and
garnish with mint. Set aside in
the refrigerator.
Brush the top of the Italian
bread with olive oil and
sprinkle on Parmesan cheese.
Wrap in aluminum foil and
bake at 350° for 15 minutes.
Bring a large pot of water to
the boil while preparing Joni
Muskovitz's clam sauce. Make
a green salad tossed with your
favorite Italian dressing. Top
with some red onion rings.

Spaghetti with Clam Sauce

¼ cup olive oil
1 clove garlic, minced
¼ cup dry white wine
3 tablespoons minced
    fresh parsley
½ teaspoon salt
black pepper to taste
¼ cup water
2 tablespoons capers
1 8-ounce can clams
    with juice
1 tablespoon butter
2 teaspoons flour
1 cup milk
crushed hot dried red
    pepper flakes to
    taste
½ pound spaghetti
grated Parmesan cheese

> In a skillet heat olive oil. Add garlic and sauté for 1 minute. Stir in wine, parsley, salt, pepper, water, capers, and clams. Cook for 5 minutes.

> In a saucepan melt butter, stir in flour, and cook for 1 minute. Gradually add milk, whisking constantly. Bring to boil, reduce to simmering, and cook for 3 minutes. Add clam mixture and red pepper flakes.

> Bring large pot of salted water to boiling. Add spaghetti. Cook according to package directions. Drain and toss with clam sauce. Serve with Parmesan cheese.

On Leftover Pasta...

I don't know about you, but I have a tendency to cook more pasta than I need. Here are some ideas about what to do with those leftover noodles:

1. *Add to soups at the end of cooking, just to heat through.*
2. *Add to chicken or meat casseroles at the end of baking time.*
3. *Add small-shaped pasta to a meat loaf mixture.*
4. *Fry in a little oil until browned and crisp and use to garnish soup or salad.*
5. *Toss the pasta with vegetables and a sesame oil vinaigrette for a vegetarian salad.*
6. *Add elbow macaroni to bottled marinated three-bean salad.*

ITALIAN NIGHT AT HOME

MENU

ANTIPASTO PLATTER

BAKED TORTELLINI

GARLIC GENOA TOASTS

SPUMONI ICE CREAM

BEVERAGE:
DRY, LIGHT-BODIED
WHITE WINE

For this menu prepare the tortellini first and put it in the oven to bake. Then, arrange the antipasto platter, choosing an assortment from the following: roasted red peppers, marinated artichoke hearts, olives, anchovies, and thinly sliced salamis. Genoa toasts are available in most supermarkets, or make your own by substituting Italian bread sliced ¼ inch thick and brushed with olive oil, toasted under the broiler. Serve spumoni ice cream for dessert.

Baked Tortellini

5½ tablespoons butter
1¼ cups heavy cream
2 tablespoons minced fresh parsley
1 pound frozen tortellini
1 cup diced tomatoes
2 ounces ham, julienned
4 ounces Italian Fontina cheese, cut into ½-inch cubes
2½ ounces goat cheese, crumbled
¼ cup grated Parmesan cheese
¼ cup bread crumbs

Preheat oven to 350°. Grease an ovenproof casserole.

In a saucepan melt 4 tablespoons butter and add cream. Bring to the boil and reduce to simmering. Cook for 10 minutes, until slightly thickened. Stir in parsley.

Bring a pot of salted water to the boil. Add frozen tortellini to pot and bring back to the boil. When tortellini rises to the surface, drain. Toss with tomatoes, ham, and Fontina. Arrange in casserole. Pour cream mixture on top and sprinkle on goat and Parmesan cheeses. Sprinkle bread crumbs on top and dot with remaining 1½ tablespoons butter. Bake for 20 minutes, until bubbling and golden brown.

On Tortellini...

Combine tortellini—some made with egg and some made with spinach pasta—for a prettier presentation. Also, tortellini is now available fresh or frozen with a variety of fillings, so why not mix up a few compatible fillings?

SAUCES

COOKING ON BORROWED TIME

Next time you find yourself with a little free time, use it wisely. Prepare sauces that freeze well and which you can pull out on a moment's notice and turn into a wonderful meal, spending only a minimal amount of cooking and shopping time. Even better yet, freeze sauces in containers appropriate for your family size, whether it is 1, 2, 3, or 4. Just pull the sauce container out of your freezer and refrigerate overnight to defrost. Or, if it's really a last-minute meal, defrost quickly in the microwave. With just one Sunday afternoon's work, you can

MENU

SALSA

PESTO

TOMATO SAUCE

STIR-FRY SAUCE

OLD-FASHIONED GRAVY

relieve yourself of the task of cooking for days. The sauce recipes here can provide you with gourmet international dinners for every night of the week.

Salsa

This sauce can be folded into omelettes or used to top scrambled or fried eggs, poached fish, or hamburgers.

1–2 jalapeño peppers
6 sprigs fresh coriander
1 small yellow onion,
    coarsely chopped
4 tomatoes, finely
    chopped
salt and pepper to taste
2⅔ cups canned tomato
    sauce
3 tablespoons chopped
    fresh parsley
5 tablespoons tomato
    paste
2½ teaspoons sugar
¾ teaspoon dried
    oregano
2½ tablespoons
    safflower oil
2½ teaspoons white
    wine vinegar

Remove stem and seeds from jalapeño pepper. Finely chop pepper and combine with coriander. Combine with onion and tomatoes in a bowl, and add salt. Place mixture in bowl of food processor fitted with steel blade, or in blender. Add remaining ingredients. Process until well blended. Heat in a 2½-quart saucepan over medium heat; let simmer for 20 minutes over medium heat. If sauce is too thick, add a little water to thin to desired consistency. Taste and adjust seasonings. *Makes approximately 6½ cups.*

Pesto

Toss with pasta cooked al dente. Pesto can also be added to scrambled eggs, potato salad, or mixed with mayonnaise for poached fish.

Place basil in bowl of food processor fitted with steel blade, or in blender. Add olive oil, nuts, and garlic; process until smooth. At this point pesto can be frozen. To serve, bring to room temperature and beat in Parmesan and butter. If desired, sauce may be heated with some heavy cream for a thinner sauce. *Makes 2 cups.*

N O T E : *This recipe can be doubled easily during the basil season. Pesto is one sauce that stays fresh in the freezer almost indefinitely.*

- 2 cups fresh basil, stems removed
- ½ cup olive oil
- 2 tablespoons pine nuts
- 2 cloves garlic
- ½ cup plus 2 tablespoons grated Parmesan cheese
- 3 tablespoons butter, softened
- heavy cream (optional)

Tomato Sauce

Serve with pasta, eggplant parmigiana, ravioli, chicken cutlets, or on pizza.

Heat olive oil in a large skillet over medium heat and add onion. Sauté until softened, about 5 minutes. Add remaining ingredients and bring to the boil. Reduce to simmering and cook, uncovered, for 30 minutes, or until sauce is thick. Puree in food processor or blender and set aside to cool. *Makes 2 cups.*

N O T E : *This may easily be made in greater quantity.*

- ½ cup olive oil
- 1 large onion, thinly sliced
- 2 pounds fresh tomatoes
- 1 tablespoon minced garlic
- ¼ cup chopped fresh basil
- 1 tablespoon chopped fresh parsley
- ½ teaspoon sugar
- 1 teaspoon salt
- black pepper to taste
- dried hot red pepper flakes to taste

STIR-FRY SAUCE

1 teaspoon chili paste
½ teaspoon ground
　ginger
½ teaspoon garlic
　powder
3 tablespoons sugar
1 teaspoon salt
6 tablespoons cider
　vinegar
6 tablespoons soy sauce
3 tablespoons dry sherry

In a bowl combine chili paste, ginger, and garlic powder. Stir to combine and add remaining ingredients. *Makes about 1 cup.*

N O T E : *To use with pork, beef, chicken, shrimp and assorted vegetables, season 1 pound meat, etc. with salt to taste. In a small bowl dissolve 1 tablespoon cornstarch in 2 tablespoons water. Stir-fry meat over high heat until cooked and add 6 tablespoons sauce. Add cornstarch mixture and bring to the boil for 1 minute to thicken sauce.*

OLD-FASHIONED GRAVY

May be served on meat loaf, liver and onions, hot roast beef or turkey sandwiches, and mashed potatoes "diner-style."

3 tablespoons meat
　drippings (see
　Note)
3 tablespoons flour
3 tablespoons Madeira
2 cups beef stock,
　warmed
salt and pepper to taste

Next time you roast beef, turkey, duck, Cornish hen, or chicken, degrease roasting pan, leaving 3 tablespoons drippings in pan. Sprinkle flour over fat in pan and blend with a wooden spoon. Cook until flour is lightly browned. Whisk in Madeira and bring to the boil. Gradually add stock and scrape up brown bits in bottom of pan. Bring to the boil, reduce heat, and simmer until thickened, about 3 minutes. Season with salt and pepper. *Makes 2 cups.*

N O T E : *If you don't have a roast, you can use butter. It will not have the same flavor, but it will be a gravy of sorts. If you have more than 3 tablespoons drippings left, increase the remaining ingredients proportionately to make extra gravy.*

*O*N FREEZING FOODS...

1. *If there is a power blackout, don't open the freezer door. If the freezer is full and remains closed, stored food should stay frozen for a day.*
2. *Wrap food tightly for freezer storage, leaving a minimum of air space.*
3. *Make sure to label all freezer packages with the contents and date.*
4. *Give hot food in a container some time to cool before you seal airtight, in order to prevent causing bacteria to develop.*

CHAPTER 4

ENTERTAINING MENUS

ANATOMY OF THE PERFECT DINNER PARTY

*F*irst you get this idea in your head that it might be nice to entertain a few friends one weekend. After you have made the phone calls (or mailed out the invitations), reality sets in. You actually have to entertain these people!

Contrary to your expectations when you extended these invitations, the "week before" has arrived and war has not broken out, nor has a plague reared its ugly head, and so now it's time to spring into action.

The most important caterer's tip I can pass on to you is to be organized. Organization and advance preparations go hand-in-hand. If you're organized and feel everything is under control, you will be the perfect confident host or hostess.

Before you plan the menu, you might want to consider choosing a theme for the evening. If you are celebrating a special event or maybe just the onset of spring, you should plan your menu accordingly.

From a timesaving point of view, the format you choose is very important. If you decide on a black-tie dinner party, you know your work is cut out for you, and that's great if you have the time and are in the mood for the work. If you go the route of an outdoor barbecue, you are entitled to use paper plates, thereby cutting down on cleanup time. You can even involve your guests in the actual cooking. If you invite a small group and choose to plate the food in the kitchen, you save time by not having to select and clean up serving platters. On the other hand, if you set out a buffet, don't forget to provide lap-size dinner napkins. Also, your menu should include foods that don't require use of a knife and aren't heavily sauced.

Beware of making an overly ambitious meal. You don't want to end up spending so much time in the kitchen that you don't have enough time to get your home in order. After all, the food is important, but it's not the only thing that counts when you're entertaining. Creating the right ambience will set the tone for the whole evening. If you decide on a simple roast for the main course, you will have more time to devote to a fancy dessert.

This is also not the time to try out a dish for the first time. The company dinner menus that follow are designed for six guests, my favorite number. These days, with space being at such a premium, a table for six can even fit in the foyer for an impromptu dinner. Think about what foods you have bought from local gourmet shops that were memorable and take advantage of them to supplement your menu.

Now you move on to one of the most important things to do—list making. First, the grocery shopping list. This should be broken down so far as to include even a map of where to go for what and the easiest "pick-up" route to save time. Then comes the plan-of-attack list, which outlines what to do each day of the week (or more) before the party. This would include buying the wine, setting the table, arranging for the flowers or other centerpiece, selecting the appropriate serving pieces, deciding on the seating arrangement of your guests, and mapping out which day to make or start each dish.

You should also consider hiring some extra help. You might want a bartender, if you're having a large group. Also consider a waiter to serve, or even someone else to finish up the cooking if there are a lot of last-minute chores. Once you have determined your needs, you may find that the employment agencies at your local high school or college are a good source for help.

The day of the party you should get an early start taking care of last-minute errands and cooking. You need to save some special time for yourself to take a long hot bath and get recycled into the party mode!

When your guests arrive, if it's an informal night, you might want to serve drinks in the kitchen and let your guests help with setting the table.

The most important rule I follow when entertaining is not to disappear into the kitchen, leaving my guests for too long or too often. Guests get uncomfortable when they think their hostess is working too hard. If you are relaxed and having a good time, chances are they will too.

FISH

COMPANY COOKOUT

MENU

GRILLED STUFFED
SWORDFISH STEAK

POTATO-CARROT
PANCAKES

ASPARAGUS WITH
LEMON VINAIGRETTE

MY MOM'S
STRAWBERRY PIE

BEVERAGE:
GIN AND TONIC

When swordfish is carefully cooked by the Canadian Fisheries method (10 minutes per inch of thickness, measured at the thickest part of the fish), there's no need to worry about it being dry. The stuffing is also extra insurance to guarantee moistness as well as extra flavor. Much of this menu can be done ahead. Prepare the swordfish stuffing the day before. Parboil the asparagus, prepare the dressing, and bake the pie shell the day before. This leaves just a few things to do on party day!

GRILLED STUFFED SWORDFISH STEAK

2¼ pounds swordfish
    steak, 1½ inches
    thick
6 tablespoons butter
2 small leeks, minced
4 shallots, minced
1 medium-size yellow
    onion, minced
8 ounces mozzarella
    cheese, cut into ½-
    inch cubes
salt and pepper to taste
olive oil
lemon wedges

Prepare coals for grilling.

Using a sharp knife, cut a pocket into the long side of the swordfish. Be sure not to cut all the way through. Set the fish aside. Melt butter in skillet and sauté leeks, shallots, and yellow onion for 5 minutes, or until softened. Set aside in a bowl to cool slightly. Add mozzarella to onions, season with salt and pepper, and using a spoon, stuff the fish pocket with onion mixture. Don't stuff too full. With kitchen string, tie 3 times around at intervals to hold in stuffing. Brush with olive oil and grill over a hot charcoal fire, turning once, or broil 4 inches from heat source for 10 minutes for each inch of thickness of fish, or about 15 minutes. Serve each portion with wedge of lemon.

POTATO-CARROT PANCAKES

¾ pound all-purpose
    potatoes, peeled
¾ pound carrots, peeled
3 eggs
3 tablespoons flour
3 tablespoons minced
    onion
½ teaspoon salt
black pepper to taste
2 tablespoons butter

In food processor fitted with a shredding disc shred potatoes and carrots into long "spidery" strands. In a bowl lightly beat eggs and add flour. Stir well to combine. Add potatoes, carrots, onion, salt, and pepper.

In a heavy skillet melt butter and drop batter by spoonfuls. Cook until browned, turn, and brown on other side (about 3 minutes per side). Drain on paper towels. *Makes approximately twenty-two 2-inch pancakes.*

Variation: When made small enough, these pancakes can be served as hors d'oeuvres.

N O T E : *May be frozen and reheated without defrosting on cookie sheet in 375° oven for 6 to 8 minutes, depending on size.*

Asparagus with Lemon Vinaigrette

Bring large pot of salted water to the boil. Add asparagus and bring water back to boiling. Boil slowly for 5 minutes, or until tender. Drain in a colander and run under cold water to cool quickly. Dry well. Set aside.

In a bowl whisk together lemon juice and salt and pepper. Slowly drizzle in olive oil, whisking constantly until dressing forms an emulsion.

To serve, arrange asparagus on salad plates. Drizzle sauce across spears in 3 rows. Garnish between one row with pimento and another row with chopped egg.

2 pounds asparagus, peeled
¼ cup lemon juice
salt and pepper to taste
¾ cup olive oil
2 teaspoons minced pimento
1 egg, hard-boiled, minced

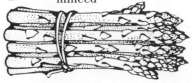

My Mom's Strawberry Pie

In a bowl combine sugar and cornstarch. Sort through berries, saving perfect ones to arrange decoratively on top. In saucepan combine remaining berries and water. Bring to the boil and boil for 3 minutes. Remove from heat and add cornstarch mixture. Stir to combine. Return to heat, bring to boil, and boil slowly for 4 minutes, or until thick. Set aside. Dip "perfect" berries into liquid to coat them.

Sprinkle a thin layer of bread crumbs on bottom of baked shell. Pour in liquid and smooth over top. Arrange "perfect" berries standing up decoratively on top.

When completely cool, use a pastry bag or spoon to decorate top with whipped cream.

¾ cup sugar
3 tablespoons cornstarch
1 quart strawberries, hulled
¾ cup water
1 tablespoon bread crumbs
single crust pastry for 9-inch pie, completely baked
1 cup whipped cream

On Fish Odors...

To remove fish odors from your hands, wash first with salt, then with cold water. Or, rub your hands with cut lemons and rinse away odors.

FRESH AND FANCY

MENU

〰〰〰 CURRIED ZUCCHINI
SOUP

ooooo HALIBUT EN
PAPILLOTE

++++++ COUSCOUS SALAD

▰▰▰▰▰ MELTAWAY
CHOCOLATE PIE

▼▼▼▼▼▼ BEVERAGE:
WHITE WINE
SPRITZER

Baking the halibut en papillote or "in paper" keeps the fish incredibly moist. The paper is traditionally made of parchment but can just as easily be aluminum foil. The fish is tightly sealed in the paper, along with the vegetable, and can be assembled ahead of time. Best of all, since the fish is served directly from the paper package, there is no mess to clean up!

The soup and salad can be prepared the day before. The halibut can be assembled in the morning and brought to room temperature before baking. The pie can be made the day before but don't garnish with whipped cream until a few hours before serving.

CURRIED ZUCCHINI SOUP

Slice zucchini into ½-inch chunks, reserving one-quarter of 1 zucchini, and place in a 2-quart saucepan. Add onion, curry powder, and stock. Bring to the boil. Reduce to simmering, cover, and cook for 20 minutes or until vegetables are soft. Puree in a blender or food processor fitted with steel blade. Add milk and process to blend thoroughly. Add salt and pepper.

Julienne reserved zucchini quarter and use to garnish at serving. Serve soup hot or cold.

5 small to medium zucchini
1 large onion, thinly sliced
½–1 teaspoon curry powder
3 cups chicken stock
1¼ cups milk
salt and pepper to taste

HALIBUT EN PAPILLOTE

Preheat oven to 500°. In a bowl or food processor mash together butter, parsley, oregano, and garlic.

Fold each rectangle of paper in half. Using a scissors, start cutting from the folded side, following an imaginary line that resembles a question mark. Open the heart shape, grease paper, and center each steak on the bottom halves. Season fish with salt and pepper and sprinkle with wine. Top fish with celery and carrots and dot with butter mixture. Lay the top paper over fish: Starting at the fold, fold the edge, overlapping on itself as you go along so fish is sealed well. May be done ahead to this point and refrigerated. Set on baking sheet and bake for 10 minutes.

Serve papillote on individual plates and have guests open their own package. Puncture top with a knife and pull back paper (be careful of escaping steam).

6 tablespoons butter, softened
6 tablespoons chopped fresh parsley
1 teaspoon dried oregano
1½ teaspoons minced garlic
6 10"-x-12" sheets of parchment or foil
6 1-inch-thick halibut steaks
salt and pepper to taste
6 tablespoons white wine
4 stalks celery, shredded
3 carrots, shredded

Couscous salad

1 cup instant couscous
2 medium cucumbers, diced
1 large tomato, diced
4 tablespoons chopped fresh parsley
1 tablespoon chopped fresh mint

VINAIGRETTE:

1 tablespoon raspberry vinegar
2 tablespoons red wine vinegar
9 tablespoons olive oil
salt and pepper to taste

Cook couscous according to package directions, omitting butter. Fluff with a fork and set aside in a bowl to cool. Then add cucumbers, tomato, parsley, and mint.

In a screw-top jar combine vinaigrette ingredients. Shake to combine and pour enough dressing over salad to moisten. Chill and serve.

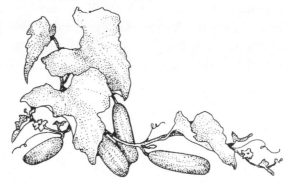

Meltaway chocolate pie

1⅔ cups graham cracker crumbs
¼ cup plus 2 tablespoons sugar
⅓ cup butter, softened
12 ounces semisweet chocolate morsels
3 tablespoons milk
4 eggs, separated
pinch salt
½ teaspoon vanilla extract
1 cup heavy cream, whipped
chocolate curls (see Sidebar)

Preheat oven to 375°.

In a bowl combine crumbs, ¼ cup sugar, and butter. Blend well with a fork. Press mixture into a 9-inch pie plate to coat bottom and sides. Bake for 8 minutes. Set on rack to cool.

In a saucepan melt chocolate morsels with 2 tablespoons sugar and milk. When smooth, set saucepan in a larger bowl of ice water to hasten cooling. When cool, add egg yolks, one at a time, beating well after each addition.

In the clean bowl of an electric mixer beat egg whites with salt until soft peaks form. Add vanilla and beat to combine. Fold chocolate mixture into egg whites. Pour into graham cracker crust. Decorate with whipped cream and chocolate curls.

ON SOUP...

1. *If desired, "beef up" canned broth by adding a carrot, stalk of celery, an unpeeled onion, and 2 parsley sprigs. Bring to the boil, reduce heat, and simmer for 15 minutes. Strain and proceed with your recipe.*

2. *When making soup stock, don't bother peeling the onions. Your stock will take on a deep rich color from the peels, and you'll have saved yourself time, too.*

3. *Use a dampened coffee filter as a substitute for cheesecloth when straining stock.*

4. *Freeze soup stock in ice-cube trays. Transfer to a plastic bag and label. Use in recipes like those in Chinese cooking that call for 1 to 2 tablespoons of stock.*

5. *When making soup, drop a lettuce leaf into the pot to absorb grease from the top of the soup. Remove and discard the lettuce when ready to serve soup.*

ON CHOCOLATE DECORATIONS...

1. *To make chocolate curls to decorate the top of cakes or pies, hold a wrapped square of unsweetened chocolate in your hand to warm slightly. Unwrap and shave with long thin strokes, using a vegetable peeler.*

2. *Use chocolate-coated orange sticks from the candy store to decorate the top of a pie. Hold a fistful over the top of the pie and let fall like pickup sticks wherever.*

SUMMER PATIO BARBECUE

MENU

~~~~
SMOKED SALMON
CORNUCOPIAS

• • • •
GRILLED TROUT
WITH COUSCOUS
STUFFING

SKEWERED WILD
MUSHROOMS

CHOCOLATE
MOUSSE CAKE

BEVERAGE:
DRY, LIGHT-
BODIED
WHITE WINE

*E*verything
about this dinner is
quick and can be cooked on the
grill while you and your guests
sip drinks and sample salmon
cornucopias on the patio. This
is the perfect time to indulge in
Susan Browse's spectacular
dessert. It takes a little time
but is well worth the effort!

Smoked Salmon Cornucopias

Serve these as an hors d'oeuvre on a tray garnished with a bed of mustard sprouts or as a first course with thinly sliced black bread.

Wrap and fold salmon into cornucopia or cigarette shape. Spoon a little horseradish sauce in the hollow formed and poke some sprouts in at the ends.

¾ pound smoked salmon, thinly sliced

4 tablespoons prepared horseradish sauce

4 ounces mustard sprouts, or any other sprouts

Grilled Trout with Couscous Stuffing

Prepare coals for grill.

In a saucepan combine 6 tablespoons butter, chicken stock, and saffron. Bring to the boil and add couscous. Cover and remove from heat. Let stand for 4 minutes. Turn into a dish and fluff with a fork. Set aside.

In a skillet melt remaining 3 tablespoons butter and sauté red pepper for 3 minutes. Season with salt and pepper. Stir into couscous. Set aside to cool.

Stuff trout with couscous mixture and tie trout closed with kitchen string. Brush with olive oil before setting on oiled grill. Grill for about 5 minutes on each side. Untie before serving.

9 tablespoons butter

3 cups chicken stock

¼ teaspoon saffron threads

3 cups "instant" couscous

1 red bell pepper, minced

salt and pepper to taste

olive oil

6 rainbow trout, boned but left whole

NOTE : *Trout may also be cooked in 2 or 3 skillets on top of the stove in a mix of butter and oil. Cook for 5 minutes on each side.*

Skewered Wild Mushrooms

24 shiitake mushrooms,
    stems removed
6 bamboo skewers
½ cup olive oil
2 cloves garlic, minced
3 tablespoons minced
    fresh parsley

Thread 4 mushrooms on each skewer. Combine olive oil, garlic, and parsley. Brush on mushrooms and grill for 5 minutes, turning occasionally, or until slightly softened.

Chocolate Mousse Cake

5½ ounces unsweetened
    chocolate
2½ ounces semisweet
    chocolate
2 sticks (1 cup) butter,
    cut into 16 pieces
8 egg yolks
1 cup plus 2 tablespoons
    sugar
5 egg whites
1 tablespoon
    unsweetened cocoa
1 teaspoon
    confectioners' sugar

Preheat oven to 350°. Grease bottom and sides of an 8-inch springform pan.

Put unsweetened and semisweet chocolate in saucepan with butter. Melt over very low heat and stir until completely smooth.

In the bowl of an electric mixer beat egg yolks, slowly adding sugar, and beat until light and lemon colored. Add melted chocolate to egg mixture and stir to blend.

In clean bowl of electric mixer beat egg whites until stiff. Stir half the whites into chocolate mixture. Using a spatula, fold in remaining whites.

Pour three-quarters of mixture into pan. Set aside remainder.

Bake for 40 minutes. Remove from oven. Release springform. Frost top and sides of cake with reserved chocolate mixture. Sieve cocoa on top and set on rack to cool completely. Sieve confectioners' sugar on top.

For elegant decoration, hold a decorative doily over top of cake and sieve powdered sugar over it to get a lacy design.

MORE ON GRILLING FISH...

1. *Cook fish quicker by cutting fish such as salmon, tuna, and swordfish into chunks. Thread on skewers and baste brochettes while cooking.*
2. *Use a hinged wire basket when cooking more delicate fish to simplify turning.*
3. *Put a piece of aluminum foil on the grill and poke a few holes in it. Arrange fish fillets skin side down on the foil and don't turn. When the fish is done, scrape the fish off the foil, leaving the skin behind to be discarded.*

ENTERTAINING THOUGHTS

When you think summer, here are some of the foods to look for at their peak in the market:

Basil	*Apricots*
Corn	*Blueberries*
Squash blossoms	*Nectarines*
Nasturtiums	*Cherries*
Squash	*Mangoes*
Tomatoes	*Local melons*
Cucumbers	*Plums*
Eggplants	*Raspberries*

SPECIAL OCCASION DINNER

MENU

\\\\\ ENDIVE, FENNEL, AND RED ONION SALAD

▪▪▪▪▪▪ FILLET OF SOLE WITH CRABMEAT SAUCE

◆◆◆◆◆ BROCCOLI WITH TOASTED PECANS

●❙●❙●❙● HOT FUDGE PUDDING CAKE

▲▲▲▲ BEVERAGE: MEDIUM FULL-BODIED WHITE WINE

This dinner is elegant enough to celebrate any special occasion. The recipe for the Hot Fudge Pudding Cake comes from Joni Muskovitz, and when I first made it, I thought to myself: This can't be right, it looks so strange. But, it is right and it is delicious!

ENDIVE, FENNEL, AND RED ONION SALAD

Trim the tops from fennel, reserving fronds and thinly slice bulbs. Place in a bowl with red onion and endive.

In a screw-top jar combine vinegar, salt and pepper, and olive oil. Pour over salad when ready to serve. Garnish with fennel fronds.

3 fennel bulbs
1 large red onion, thinly sliced
4 endive, sliced on the diagonal into rings
3 tablespoons red wine vinegar
salt and pepper to taste
9 tablespoons olive oil

FILLET OF SOLE WITH CRABMEAT SAUCE

Preheat oven to 350°. Grease a shallow casserole.

In a saucepan melt 2 tablespoons butter. Add flour and stir for 1 minute. Add salt, ¾ teaspoon lemon juice, horseradish, Worcestershire, hot pepper sauce, and pepper. Slowly whisk in milk and cook, stirring, until thickened. Remove from heat and add crabmeat.

Arrange fillets in a single layer in casserole. Pour crabmeat sauce over fish.

In a bowl combine bread crumbs, 3 tablespoons melted butter, and remaining 2 teaspoons lemon juice. Sprinkle bread crumb mixture on top of fillets. Bake for 30 minutes.

2 tablespoons butter
1½ tablespoons flour
½ teaspoon salt
2¾ teaspoons lemon juice
½ teaspoon bottled horseradish, drained
¼ teaspoon Worcestershire sauce
⅛ teaspoon hot pepper sauce
black pepper to taste
½ cup milk
1½ cups crabmeat
2¼ pounds fillet of sole
½ cup bread crumbs
3 tablespoons butter, melted

N O T E : *May be assembled ahead of time. Prepare sauce and set aside to cool before assembling. Bring to room temperature before baking.*

BROCCOLI WITH TOASTED PECANS

2 bunches broccoli
1 stick (½ cup) butter
4 ounces pecans, finely
    chopped (1 cup)
salt and pepper to taste

Trim off florets from stems. Peel stems and dice. Bring pot of salted water to the boil, add broccoli and cook for about 5 minutes, or until tender. Drain. (May be prepared ahead to this point.)

In a skillet melt butter and add pecans. Cook until lightly browned, about 10 minutes. Add broccoli and heat through. Season with salt and pepper.

HOT FUDGE PUDDING CAKE

1 cup flour
⅔ cup white sugar
½ cup unsweetened
    cocoa
2 teaspoons baking
    powder
¼ teaspoon salt
½ cup milk
¼ cup vegetable oil
1 teaspoon vanilla
    extract
¼ cup brown sugar
1¾ cups hot water

This cake looks awful but tastes great!

Preheat oven to 350°. Grease a 9-inch square pan.

In a bowl combine flour, white sugar, ¼ cup cocoa, baking powder, and salt. Stir until smooth. Add milk, oil, and vanilla. Stir to combine. Pour into pan. There is not very much batter, but spread in a thin layer.

In a small bowl combine brown sugar and remaining ¼ cup cocoa. Sprinkle over batter in pan. Pour hot water evenly over batter. Do not stir. Bake for 45 minutes. It will be gooey.

Cut into squares and serve warm with vanilla ice cream.

CENTERPIECE FROM THE GARDEN

Take a walk in your garden (or by the side of the road) in summer and winter. Shrubs and plants take on a completely different look when they are bare, flowering, or leafed out. For instance, a branch of contorta (commonly known as "walking stick") clipped in the winter is very sculptural and can stand alone in a vase or be combined with other flowers. Any of the following would make a graceful centerpiece:

Rhododendron flower floating in a
  large brandy snifter
Branch of flowering
  dogwood
Branch of weeping cherry
Winter branch of contorta
Branch of holly berries
Assorted evergreens
Snippets of boxwood
Black-eyed Susans
Hosta leaves
Pots of herbs
Pinecones
Ferns

VIP

DINNER

MENU

SWEET AND SOUR
EGG SOUP

STIR-FRIED SHRIMP
WITH VEGETABLES

MY VERSION OF
CHINESE RICE

LEMON SHERBET

PECAN SANDIES

BEVERAGE:
TEA OR
CHINESE BEER

My mother used to make this Sweet and Sour Egg Soup when I was a child and I loved seeing the egg floating in it. I had quite a time trying to remember how to make it to include here—but I think I have done it.

For this Chinese dinner pull out your chopsticks and any other oriental decorative accents you have to set a pretty table.

Buy the smoothest lemon sherbet you can find to serve for dessert.

SWEET AND SOUR EGG SOUP

In a 1½- to 2-quart saucepan melt butter. Add flour, stir to combine, and cook over medium to high heat, stirring constantly, until roux (butter mixture) is lightly browned. Slowly whisk in water and stir constantly until smooth. Add salt, vinegar, and sugar. Bring soup to the boil.

After soup comes to the boil, carefully crack eggs directly into soup. Try to keep them separate. As the egg cooks, it will solidify like a poached egg. Reduce heat to simmering and cook for 20 minutes. Taste and adjust seasonings. Garnish each serving with an egg.

4 tablespoons butter
4 tablespoons flour
3 cups water
¼ teaspoon salt
2 tablespoons white
    vinegar
4 teaspoons sugar
6 eggs

STIR-FRIED SHRIMP WITH VEGETABLES

In a small bowl combine soy sauce, Scotch, sesame oil, and stock. Add sugar and salt and stir.

In a skillet heat oil. When hot add shrimp and cook, turning once, for 1 minute, or until just pink. Remove to a bowl and add garlic and green onions to skillet. Sauté for 30 seconds. Add soy sauce mixture, snow peas, corn, and shrimp. Cook, stirring for 1 minute to combine flavors.

Arrange Chinese rice in a bowl and mound shrimp and vegetables in center. Serve with chopsticks.

3 tablespoons soy sauce
¼ cup Scotch whisky
1 tablespoon sesame oil
½ cup plus 2
    tablespoons
    chicken stock
½ teaspoon sugar
salt to taste
3 tablespoons peanut oil
2½ pounds medium raw
    shrimp, peeled and
    deveined
1½ teaspoons minced
    garlic
1 bunch green onions,
    thinly sliced
1 pound pea pods, or 2
    6-ounce packages
    frozen (thawed)
1½ cups canned baby
    corn, drained

My Version of Chinese Rice

1½ cups long-grain rice
water

Put rice in a 1½-quart saucepan. Add enough water to come 1 inch above top of rice. Bring to the boil and boil slowly, until all water has been absorbed and crater holes appear on top of rice. You may set aside rice, covered, for up to 20 minutes. Fluff with a fork and serve with shrimp.

Pecan Sandies

1 stick (½ cup) butter, softened
2 tablespoons confectioners' sugar
1 cup flour
¾ teaspoon cold water
½ teaspoon vanilla extract
½ cup chopped pecans

Preheat oven to 325°.

In a bowl of an electric mixer cream together butter and confectioners' sugar. Add flour and cold water. Blend well. Add vanilla and pecans. Stir to combine. Roll dough between palms of hands into walnut-size balls. Place on ungreased baking sheet 2 inches apart. Bake for 15 minutes. Cool on wire rack. Roll in additional confectioners' sugar. *Makes 3 dozen.*

On Making Tea...

Bring a kettle of cold water to the boil.
Rinse out a porcelain or earthenware teapot with some of the hot water.
Measure about 1 teaspoon dried leaves (or 1 teabag) per cup.
Place in the teapot and add the boiling water. Cover and let steep for about 3 to 5 minutes. Strain and serve.

Entertaining Thoughts

There are so many beautiful place mats available now in stores, but why not try to use something a little different. For instance, substitute a large fern leaf, large philodendron monstera leaf, 14-inch round or square doilies, pretty kitchen towels, or bamboo mats.

THE HEAT'S ON

MENU

CORN TORTILLA
WITH CRABMEAT
AND GUACAMOLE

ooooo

ORANGE SALAD
WITH RED ONION
RINGS

▲▲▲▲▲

MANGOES WITH
STRAWBERRY SAUCE

MANGOES WITH
STRAWBERRY SAUCE

BEVERAGE:
FIREWATER

*W*hen the heat is on outside who wants to turn the oven on and heat up the kitchen inside? This spicy tortilla dish is prepared all in one bowl for easy cleanup. The tortillas can be briefly warmed in the toaster oven or microwave (wrap in dampened paper towel and heat on HIGH for 30 seconds).

CORN TORTILLA WITH CRABMEAT AND GUACAMOLE

GUACAMOLE:

1½ packages frozen corn, thawed
3 large avocados, peeled and diced (see Note)
6 tablespoons minced fresh coriander
3 cloves garlic, minced
½ cup diced tomato
6 tablespoons minced red onion
3 jalapeño peppers, stemmed, seeded, and minced
3 tablespoons lime juice
3 tablespoons olive oil
salt and pepper to taste

6 corn tortillas, warmed
6 cups chopped mixed greens
1½ pounds crabmeat, flaked

In a bowl combine corn, avocados, coriander, garlic, tomato, red onion, jalapeño peppers, lime juice, olive oil, salt and pepper. Using the back of a fork, lightly mash the ingredients together. The mixture should be chunky and not a puree.

To serve, place warmed tortilla on each plate, sprinkle with a handful of greens. Place a mound of guacamole in center and surround with crabmeat.

Variation: For an hors d'oeuvre, serve the guacamole with jícama sticks and taco chips instead of crabmeat and tortillas.

N O T E : *Haas dark green, almost black-skinned, avocados are the best.*

MANGOES WITH STRAWBERRY SAUCE

6 mangoes, peeled
1½ pounds strawberries, hulled, plus 12 whole strawberries
¾ cup sugar
6 tablespoons Kahlúa

Cut mangoes in half. Set aside.

In a food processor or blender puree hulled strawberries, sugar, and Kahlúa.

Spoon some sauce on bottom of dessert plate. Place 2 mango halves on top, drizzle with some additional sauce, and garnish each mango half with whole strawberry.

ORANGE SALAD WITH RED ONION RINGS

Arrange lettuce leaves on individual salad plates. Place oranges in circular fashion on top of lettuce. Mound onion rings on top.

In screw-top jar combine vinegar, oil, coriander, and pepper. Shake to combine. Drizzle on top of salad.

1 head of Boston lettuce
4 large navel oranges, peeled and sliced
1 large red onion, thinly sliced

VINAIGRETTE:

6 tablespoons red wine vinegar
¾ cup olive oil
3 tablespoons minced coriander
black pepper to taste

FIREWATER

6 ounces beer
1 ounce pepper vodka (pepper-flavored vodka, made by Stolichnaya and other companies)
1 lime slice

In a 10-ounce glass pour beer over ice. Float vodka over top and place lime slice on top of that. *Serves 1.*

ON CORIANDER...

I can't think of any other herb that goes by so many different names—coriander, Chinese parsley, cilantro. It will help to know them on your next trip to the market. But keep one thing in mind, don't substitute dried for the fresh variety. The flavor just isn't there. I think coriander is an acquired taste, start with a small amount and build up, until you are used to the flavor.

ON AVOCADOS...

1. *When making guacamole, save the avocado pit and bury it in the bowl to keep the guacamole from turning brown.*
2. *Spoon the guacamole into raw mushroom caps or cherry tomatoes for hors d'oeuvres.*
3. *For a first course, slice avocado into wedges on a plate and lay ribbons of prosciutto on top.*
4. *Serve guacamole on top of grilled hamburgers.*
5. *Stuff an avocado half with hot chili, a dollop of sour cream, and chopped onions.*

AFTERTHEATER SUPPER

MENU

vvvv **YELLOW SQUASH CANAPÉS**

||●||●||●||● **CRAB VOL-AU-VENT**

············ **MIXED GREENS SALAD**

~~~ **FRUIT-FILLED MELON BOWLS**

■■■■■■ **LACE COOKIES**

o o o **BEVERAGE: DRY, MEDIUM-BODIED WHITE WINE**

The canapés for this menu can be prepared ahead and set aside in the refrigerator, ready to pull out when you walk in with your guests after the theater.

The main-course patty shells and filling can be prepared ahead to be reheated. The salad ingredients can be combined ahead to be tossed at serving time. I like to put the greens in a bowl and cover with a damp paper towel (if they don't have too long to wait).

The melon bowls can be waiting in the refrigerator.

YELLOW SQUASH CANAPÉS

Place a spoonful of tapenade on top of each squash canapé. Place a parsley leaf on top. Arrange on a platter on a bed of parsley.

2 yellow summer
squash, unpeeled,
sliced ¼ inch thick
bottled tapenade
flat leaf parsley

CRAB VOL-AU-VENT

Bake patty shells according to package directions. Melt butter in a saucepan and sauté onion for 5 minutes, without browning. Add flour and cook, stirring constantly, for 1 minute. Add soup and slowly whisk in milk. Continue to cook until mixture is smooth. Add crabmeat, sherry, parsley, and pepper. Put 1 patty shell on each plate and fill with crabmeat mixture.

6 frozen Pepperidge
Farm patty shells
6 tablespoons butter
½ cup minced onion
6 tablespoons flour
2 10½-ounce cans
cream of shrimp soup
1 cup milk
2 7½-ounce cans
crabmeat, flaked,
or 1 pound fresh
¼ cup dry sherry
6 tablespoons chopped
fresh parsley
white pepper to taste

ON PUFF PASTRY...

It used to be that recipes calling for puff pastry shells were just out of the question for some cooks. Now that's no longer true. Puff pastry can now be bought in the freezer case and just requires an overnight stay in the refrigerator to defrost. It can be used for hors d'oeuvres that are assembled and frozen ahead of time, baked as needed. It can also be used as a topper for potpies and for scrumptious fruit tarts.

MIXED GREENS SALAD

VINAIGRETTE:

1½ tablespoons sherry
    wine vinegar
2 teaspoons minced shallots
salt and pepper to taste
¼ cup olive oil
1 tablespoon walnut oil

1 small bunch arugula
1 head of radicchio
1 endive, sliced in rings
1 head of red leaf lettuce
4 ounces mâche (see Notes)

In a screw-top jar combine vinegar, shallots, salt and pepper, olive and walnut oils. Shake to combine.

Clean and dry the greens, then arrange in a salad bowl. Toss with vinaigrette.

NOTES:

You can vary salad greens according to the best of what is available.

Mâche is also called corn salad or field salad and can be bought in season at a greengrocer.

FRUIT-FILLED MELON BOWLS

There are so many different and unusual types of melon available. One melon will serve 2 people, so pick the size accordingly.

3 melons in season
3 cups of assorted fruits:
   strawberries, plums,
   grapes, blueberries,
   nectarines, peaches,
   raspberries, in season
1 tablespoon sugar
3 tablespoons brandy
6 mint sprigs

Cut melons in half and scoop out seeds and fibers. With a melon-ball cutter scoop out the flesh, leaving a ¼-inch shell.

In a bowl combine melon balls and a selection of the above fruits. Toss to combine and flavor with sugar and brandy.

Spoon back into shells and refrigerate until serving time. Garnish with mint sprigs and serve with bakery lace cookies.

ON PICKING THE PERFECT MELON...

Picking the perfect melon is an art, but it's one that can be easily learned. Avoid melons that feel mushy, have shriveled skins, or smell musty. All melons should be heavy for their size. The final important test is to sniff the blossom end of the melon. If it is ready to eat, you will smell a wonderful fragrance. The melon is overripe if the fragrance is too intense or hints of fermentation. Serve at room temperature for best flavor.

SCALLOPED SCALLOP DINNER

MENU

ENDIVE BOATS

SCALLOPED SCALLOPS

ZUCCHINI GRATIN

DOUBLE RAZZ DESSERT

BEVERAGE: DRY, MEDIUM-BODIED WHITE WINE

*F*or this dinner, the endive boats may be prepared several hours ahead and served in the living room with drinks, thereby eliminating a first course.
The zucchini and scallops can be assembled ahead of time, as well as the raspberry sauce for dessert.

ENDIVE BOATS

2 endives
2 tablespoons Chinese
 plum sauce
4 ounces smoked trout
fresh dill

Separate endive leaves. Top with a small spoonful of plum sauce and arrange a chevron of trout on top garnished with a sprig of dill. Arrange decoratively on a serving platter on a bed of fresh dill.

OTHER FILLINGS FOR ENDIVE BOATS...

Endive leaves act as a great carrier for a variety of fillings. They are easier than pastry or phyllo hors d'oeuvres to make and, as an added bonus, have fewer calories!

Where appropriate, decoratively pipe filling in leaf with a pastry bag:

· *softened cream cheese topped with a few grains of salmon caviar*
· *Boursin cheese, garnished with a bit of parsley*
· *salmon mousse, garnished with dill sprig*
· *taramasalata*
· *mixture of half blue cheese and half cream cheese, garnished with mustard cress or radish sprouts.*

ZUCCHINI GRATIN

3 medium zucchini,
 sliced ⅛ inch thick
2 tomatoes, thinly sliced
2 tablespoons minced
 fresh basil or
 oregano
¼ cup grated Parmesan
 cheese
salt and pepper to taste
3 tablespoons olive oil

Preheat oven to 350°. Grease a gratin dish.

Arrange zucchini and tomato in the dish, alternating the slices. Sprinkle on basil or oregano, Parmesan, salt and pepper. Drizzle olive oil on top and bake for 30 minutes.

Variation: Use above recipe as a topping for pizza, using store-bought bread dough.

Scalloped Scallops

Preheat broiler. Grease a shallow dish. If using sea scallops, cut them in half.

In a saucepan bring wine to the boil. Add scallops and reduce to simmering. Cook for 5 minutes. Drain scallops, reserving liquid. In same saucepan melt butter. Sauté shallots and mushrooms for 3 to 5 minutes, until softened. Stir in flour and cook for 1 minute. Slowly add reserved liquid and cream, whisking constantly until smooth. Bring to the boil. Stir until thickened. Remove from heat and add scallops and parsley. Spoon mixture into prepared dish and top with bread crumbs. Brown lightly under broiler.

Variation: Spoon mixture into individual shell-shaped ramekins for a prettier presentation. Put one ramekin on each plate.

2¼ pounds bay or sea scallops
2 cups dry white wine
¼ cup butter
¼ cup minced shallots
2½ cups sliced mushrooms (about ½ pound)
2 tablespoons flour
2 tablespoons heavy cream
2 tablespoons minced fresh parsley
½ cup buttered bread crumbs

Double Razz Dessert

Process frozen berries in a food processor fitted with a steel blade. When pureed, add kirsch. Process until smooth. Scoop sherbet into goblets and spoon sauce on top, passing additional sauce.

1 10-ounce package frozen raspberries
¼ cup kirsch
1½ pints raspberry sherbet

Barbecued Brochette Dinner

MENU

SCALLOP AND
PEPPER BROCHETTES

HERBED POTATO
PACKETS

CUCUMBERS AND
ONIONS

BLUEBERRY
PIE À LA MODE

BEVERAGE:
CHILLED DRY ROSÉ

First things first in orchestrating this menu. That means getting the fire started (or preheating the broiler) so the grill will have time to heat up while you assemble the rest of the meal. Prepare cucumbers the day before to develop the flavor. The pie may also be made a day ahead, the sorbet added just before serving.

SCALLOP AND PEPPER BROCHETTES

Prepare hot coals for grill. Thread scallops and peppers, alternating, on skewers.

In a saucepan add orange juice and green onions. Bring to the boil and cook until reduced to ¾ cup. Remove from heat and add butter, tomatoes, salt and pepper. Set aside to melt butter.

Brush brochettes with olive oil and grill for about 10 minutes, turning occasionally and brushing with additional oil. Serve on skewer with sauce and a sprinkling of parsley.

2¼ pounds sea scallops
2 red bell peppers, cut into 2-inch squares
2 yellow bell peppers, cut into 2-inch squares
1¾ cups orange juice
¾ cup chopped green onions
6 tablespoons butter
¾ cup diced tomatoes
salt and pepper to taste
3 tablespoons olive oil
2 tablespoons minced fresh parsley

HERBED POTATO PACKETS

Preheat oven to 400°. Lightly butter foil.

Slice potatoes ¼ inch thick. Sprinkle with salt and pepper. Dot with butter. Tuck in a sprig thyme or rosemary and sprinkle on lemon zest. Close and seal foil tightly. Grill, or bake in oven, for about 25 minutes.

6 squares aluminum foil
12 baby new potatoes, unpeeled
salt and pepper to taste
3 tablespoons butter
sprig thyme or rosemary
1½ teaspoons lemon zest

CUCUMBERS AND ONIONS

In a bowl combine cucumbers and onions. Cover with cold water. Add remaining ingredients. Taste and adjust seasonings. Serve in small bowls as a side dish with a little of the "juice."

3 cucumbers, peeled, sliced ⅛ inch thick
2 onions, thinly sliced
5 tablespoons white vinegar
2 tablespoons sugar
salt and pepper to taste
pinch paprika

174

BLUEBERRY PIE À LA MODE

pastry for 2-crust 9-inch
pie
2 pints fresh blueberries
1 tablespoon lemon
juice
¾ cup sugar
¼ cup flour
¼ teaspoon ground
cinnamon
pinch grated nutmeg
pinch ground cloves
grated rind of 1 lemon
2 tablespoons butter
1 egg yolk beaten with 1
tablespoon water
1 quart lemon sorbet

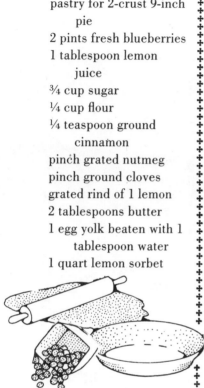

On a lightly floured surface roll half of pastry into an 11-inch circle. Press it into a 9-inch pie plate. Refrigerate remaining pastry until ready to use.

Preheat oven to 400°. Wash blueberries, drain well, and place in a bowl. Sprinkle with lemon juice.

In another bowl combine sugar, flour, cinnamon, nutmeg, cloves, and lemon rind. Add to berries and toss lightly. Turn into pie shell. Dot with butter.

Roll out remaining pastry into an 11-inch circle. Make several slits near center in order to allow steam to escape. Center pastry over filling. Fold edge of top crust under bottom crust, press together to seal, and make a decorative edge. Brush yolk and water over top crust. Bake for 45 minutes, or until juices are bubbling and crust is golden brown. Remove from oven and set aside to cool before serving.

Serve with a scoop of lemon sorbet.

HOW TO CANNELLATE A CUCUMBER...

I like to select the long, thin "gourmet" cucumbers, since it is not necessary to peel the skins. Score the skin lengthwise with the tines of a fork or use a "stripper." This can also be done to lemon slices to make an attractive garnish.

THE NEW WOMAN   FAST AND FABULOUS MENU COOKBOOK

ON GRILLING...

1. *To simplify charcoal grill cleanup, line the bottom of the grill with heavy-duty aluminum foil before adding the charcoal. After you are through grilling, lift out the foil and discard the ashes. The foil will also help the food to cook quicker.*

2. *To shorten the barbecuing time of root vegetables (potatoes, turnips, etc.), parboil or precook them a few minutes in the microwave before grilling. The same also applies to large cuts of chicken and meat.*

3. *If you're in a hurry, use a covered cooker. Keeping the lid on will speed up cooking time and reduce flare-ups.*

4. *Choose small cuts of meat for grilling meals in a hurry. Larger cuts need longer cooking times.*

5. *Brush vegetable oil on the cooking grid before use to avoid sticking.*

ENTERTAINING THOUGHTS

Grilling is a great way to involve your guests. Let them grill their own skewered dishes to the doneness they like.

POULTRY

JANICE'S CURRY-IN-A-HURRY DINNER

MENU

CHICKEN CURRY-IN-A-HURRY

RICE WITH ALMONDS AND RAISINS

CUCUMBER RAITA

COCONUT ICE CREAM WITH MARS BARS CHOCOLATE SAUCE

BEVERAGE: ICY COLD BEER

*H*ere's an Indian feast that's surprisingly simple and fast. I like my curry with a bit of bite, but you can adjust the seasonings to your taste. The sweet fruit in the curry and the tangy cool yogurt with cucumbers help offset the spices.

CHICKEN CURRY-IN-A-HURRY

Cut chicken breasts into 1-inch cubes and sprinkle with salt and pepper. In a skillet heat 3 tablespoons butter and add chicken. Cook until it loses its pink color, about 5 minutes. Remove from pan. Add remaining 3 tablespoons butter. Sauté onion and garlic until transparent.

Add curry powder, ginger, and flour. Stir to combine. Gradually add chicken broth. Bring to a boil. Reduce to simmering and add apples, bananas, and chicken. Cover and simmer for 10 to 15 minutes.

2 pounds boneless,
    skinless chicken
    breasts
salt and pepper to taste
6 tablespoons butter
1 cup chopped onion
2 garlic cloves, minced
3–4 tablespoons curry
    powder, or to taste
½ teaspoon ground
    ginger
4 tablespoons flour
3 cups chicken broth
2 apples, cored, peeled,
    and coarsely
    chopped
2 medium-large
    bananas, coarsely
    chopped

ON CURRY POWDER...

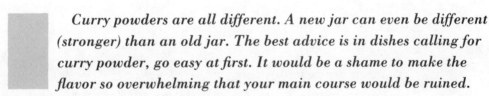

Curry powders are all different. A new jar can even be different (stronger) than an old jar. The best advice is in dishes calling for curry powder, go easy at first. It would be a shame to make the flavor so overwhelming that your main course would be ruined.

RICE WITH ALMONDS AND RAISINS

In a 2-quart saucepan melt butter. Add onion and cook until softened, about 5 minutes. Add rice, almonds, raisins, and cinnamon stick. Add chicken stock, salt and pepper. Bring to the boil and reduce to simmering. Cover and cook on low heat for 17 minutes, or until stock has been absorbed. You may set rice aside for up to 20 minutes, covered. It will become more tender. Remove cinnamon stick before serving.

4 tablespoons butter
¼ cup minced onion
1½ cups long-grain rice
5 ounces slivered
    almonds
½ cup seedless raisins
1 cinnamon stick
3 cups boiling chicken
    stock
salt and pepper to taste

CUCUMBER RAITA

3 medium cucumbers,
  peeled, cut into ⅛-
  inch-thick slices
2 cups plain yogurt
½ teaspoon salt
¾ teaspoon ground
  cumin
1½ teaspoons chopped
  fresh mint

In a bowl combine all ingredients and chill for at least two hours before serving.

COCONUT ICE CREAM WITH MARS BARS CHOCOLATE SAUCE

6 Mars bars
1 quart coconut ice
  cream
unsweetened shredded
  coconut

In top of double boiler melt Mars bars over low heat. When smooth, serve as topping for scoops of coconut ice cream. Garnish with shredded coconut.

ON BEERS...

There are so many different kinds of beers available now, why not offer an interesting variety so your guests can discover some new ones?

ENTERTAINING THOUGHTS

Some people might think place cards are a bit formal, but it makes the host or hostess pay attention ahead of time to whom he or she wants to sit where. One of my pet peeves is standing around the dinner table waiting for the hostess to decide where everyone should sit. Beautiful place cards are an added decorative element for the table. I pick them up whenever I see interesting ones and keep them tucked away in a party box.

SUNDAY KITCHEN SUPPER

MENU

ZESTY CHICKEN AND
SHRIMP RAGOUT   • • • •

GREEN RICE (PAGE
191)   ▲ ▲ ▲

GRATINÉED FENNEL   ∼∼∼

PAPAYA WITH RUM
AND LIME   ▮▮▮▮▮▮

BEVERAGE:
CHILLED DRY ROSÉ   ❖❖❖❖❖

Since this main course is a little more time-consuming than most, I like to serve it in the winter. When it's snowing and blustery outside, I find it's a perfect time to be in a warm kitchen cooking. To save time, however, the sauce for the ragout can be made ahead and even frozen. Sunday nights can be more informal than Saturday, so why not serve dinner casually with a buffet set out in the kitchen. Have lots of glowing candlelight.

ZESTY CHICKEN AND SHRIMP RAGOUT

SAUCE:

2 tablespoons butter
⅔ cup minced onions
¾ teaspoon minced
    garlic
⅓ cup minced celery
⅓ cup minced carrots
4 teaspoons flour
⅔ cup white wine
⅔ cup clam juice
3⅓ cups crushed Italian
    tomatoes
4 teaspoons tomato
    paste
½ teaspoon dried thyme
½ bay leaf
½ teaspoon dried
    tarragon
pinch cayenne pepper
salt and pepper to taste

1½ pounds boneless,
    skinless chicken
    breasts
salt and pepper to taste
5⅓ tablespoons butter
1½ pounds raw shrimp,
    shelled and
    deveined
¼ cup Cognac
3 tablespoons minced
    fresh parsley
2 teaspoons dried
    tarragon
4 teaspoons cornstarch

In a large saucepan melt butter. Add onions, garlic, celery, and carrots. Cook for 5 minutes over medium heat, until softened. Add flour, stir, and cook for 1 minute. Add remaining sauce ingredients and bring to the boil. Reduce to simmering and cook for 20 minutes. Remove bay leaf. Puree in a food processor or blender. (May be made ahead and frozen.)

Slice chicken into 1-inch cubes and season with salt and pepper. In a large skillet melt 3 tablespoons butter. Add chicken and cook until it turns white. Remove from pan and set aside. (This may have to be done in batches.)

Melt remaining 2⅓ tablespoons butter in same skillet, add shrimp, and sauté until pink. Remove and set aside. Add 2 tablespoons Cognac, 4 cups sauce, parsley, and tarragon. Bring to the boil.

In a bowl dissolve cornstarch in remaining 2 tablespoons Cognac. Add to skillet and boil gently until thickened. Return chicken and shrimp to pan to heat through.

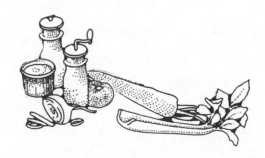

Gratinéed Fennel

Preheat oven to 375°. Butter a gratin dish.

Remove fronds from fennel bulbs and set aside "feathers" for garnish. Trim bulbs and cut into ¼-inch-thick slices. In a large skillet melt 4 tablespoons butter. Add onions and sauté for 3 minutes. Add fennel slices and salt and pepper to taste. Toss to coat with butter. Add chicken stock and bring to the boil. Reduce heat to simmering, cover, and cook for 15 minutes.

Using a slotted spoon remove vegetable mixture to gratin dish. Spoon 3 tablespoons of liquid mixture remaining in pan over vegetables. Top with Parmesan and dot with remaining 2 tablespoons butter. Bake for 10 to 15 minutes, until top is lightly browned. Garnish with fennel "feathers."

5 medium fennel bulbs
6 tablespoons butter
2 small yellow onions, thinly sliced
salt and pepper to taste
1½ cups chicken stock
½ cup grated Parmesan cheese

Papaya with Rum and Lime

Peel papayas and halve lengthwise. Remove seeds. Slice flesh lengthwise starting ½ inch from narrow end, leaving attached at stem end. Fan slices out on each dessert plate.

Grate zest from lime and reserve. Slice limes into wedges. Top papaya with a sprinkle of rum. Arrange pistachios and lime zest on top. Serve with a wedge of lime.

3 large papayas
3 limes
5 tablespoons Myers's dark rum
6 tablespoons chopped pistachios

*E*NTERING THOUGHTS

Menu planning is the short order cook's secret weapon. Keep in mind a few simple tips: If you are making a time-consuming main course, go easy on the dessert, and vice versa. Fancy main courses usually can be made in part or in whole ahead of time. Make sure to take advantage of that whenever possible. Also, remember to make use of the great things available by take-out to supplement your menu. It's also acceptable to serve hors d'oeuvres instead of a first course or, serve your first course with drinks and eliminate hors d'oeuvres. This way, you don't have an extra course to clear from the table and, if you are serving buffet-style, you don't have to sit down for the first course and then get up to get in line for the buffet!

WOK DINNER

MENU

BEAN SPROUTS WITH
SOY DRESSING ▲▲▲▲▲

WALNUT CHICKEN ℓℓℓℓℓ

STEAMED RICE ❖❖❖❖❖

PEA PODS WITH
WATER CHESTNUTS
AND STRAW
MUSHROOMS ∼∼

GREEN TEA ICE
CREAM AND
FORTUNE COOKIES ●●●●

BEVERAGE:
JASMINE TEA,
CHINESE BEER ∧∧∧

Chinese or wok cooking is a good way to involve your guests in the kitchen. The preparation or chopping is what takes some time, so divide up the tasks among friends. The cooking by you, the "star chef," takes practically no time. Serve an appropriate Chinese beer in the kitchen. Maybe even have a tasting with a few different kinds.

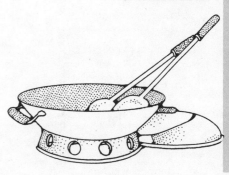

Bean sprouts with soy dressing

DRESSING:

¼ cup cider vinegar
¼ cup soy sauce
4 teaspoons peanut oil
½ teaspoon ground
 ginger
1 teaspoon sugar

½ cup green onions
 (white parts only),
 thinly sliced
2 pounds fresh bean
 sprouts or canned
 (see Note)

In a large bowl combine vinegar, soy sauce, peanut oil, ginger, and sugar. Add green onions and sprouts. Toss to combine.

N O T E : *If using canned bean sprouts, rinse and drain them first.*

Walnut chicken

5 tablespoons soy sauce
1½ tablespoons dry
 sherry
¾ teaspoon ground
 ginger
1½ pounds boneless,
 skinless chicken
 breasts, cut into 1-
 inch cubes
5 tablespoons vegetable
 oil
½ cup thinly sliced
 green onions
2 small garlic cloves,
 crushed
1½ cups coarsely
 chopped walnuts

In a bowl combine soy sauce, sherry, and ginger. Add chicken and let marinate for 15 minutes. Heat wok or skillet and add 3 tablespoons vegetable oil. Add green onions, garlic, and walnuts. Cook, stirring for 3 minutes. Remove from pan and set aside. Add remaining 2 tablespoons vegetable oil. When hot, add chicken and soy marinade. Cook, flipping and tossing chicken until done, about 5 minutes. Add walnut mixture, toss to combine, and serve.

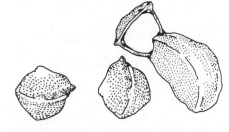

Pea Pods with Water Chestnuts and Straw Mushrooms

Heat skillet or wok over high heat for 30 seconds. Add oil and garlic, and heat for 30 seconds more. Add pea pods and flip about for 1 minute. Add remaining ingredients, cover, and cook for 1 minute.

3 tablespoons vegetable oil
1 large clove garlic, minced
¾ pound fresh pea pods
1 8-ounce can water chestnuts, drained and quartered
1 16-ounce can straw mushrooms, drained
pinch sugar
2 tablespoons soy sauce
salt and pepper to taste

Green Tea Ice Cream and Fortune Cookies

For dessert stop at your favorite Chinese restaurant and take out 1½ pints of green tea ice cream and handfuls of fortune cookies.

Entertaining Thoughts

Theme dinners are always great fun, and since this menu is so easy, devote your time to setting a spectacular table. Oriental gift shops or food markets are great places to find inexpensive bamboo place mats and chopsticks. You might even want to use individual bowls to serve rice, just the way the Chinese do.

WINTER COMFORT FOOD DINNER

MENU

CHICKEN POTPIE

CURLY LETTUCE
SALAD WITH
GRUYÈRE AND
WALNUTS

CARAMEL BANANAS

BEVERAGE:
BLOODY MARYS

The chicken potpie in this menu is a great way to use up leftover roast chicken. It can all be assembled and ready to pop in the oven before you sit down to dinner. You might even make individual potpies in 5-inch foil pie pans and keep them in the freezer for weeknight meals.

In the winter, when it is hard to get many fruits, bananas are always a good choice.

This meal is casual enough that you might want to serve it in the kitchen.

CHICKEN POTPIE

In a large saucepan melt butter. Add mushrooms and onion and sauté for 5 minutes. When softened, add flour. Cook, while stirring, for 1 minute. Slowly whisk in chicken stock. Bring to the boil to thicken, then reduce to simmering. Add Cognac, tarragon, salt and pepper, and crème fraîche. Simmer for 5 minutes. Remove from heat and add parsley, chicken, and carrots. Pour into a 10-inch Pyrex pie plate. Set aside.

Preheat oven to 450°. Roll out pastry on a lightly floured board to an 11-inch round. Pat cold water on rim of pie plate. Lay pastry on top of chicken mixture. Fold overhanging pastry on top of itself on rim to form a decorative border. Paint top with egg wash and cut steam vents in top. Bake for 20 minutes. Reduce temperature to 350° and bake for 15 minutes more.
Variation: Substitute turkey for chicken.

7 tablespoons butter
¾ pound mushrooms, sliced
1 yellow onion, sliced
6 tablespoons flour
3 cups chicken stock
3 tablespoons Cognac
1 tablespoon dried tarragon
salt and pepper to taste
3 tablespoons crème fraîche or heavy cream
3 tablespoons chopped fresh parsley
3 cups cooked chicken, cut into 1-inch pieces
4 carrots, peeled, sliced, and cooked
pastry for 1 10-inch crust
1 egg mixed with 1 teaspoon water

LORENZO'S PERFECT BLOODY MARY

1½ ounces vodka

6 ounces tomato juice

¾ teaspoon lemon juice

¼ teaspoon prepared horseradish

¼ teaspoon Worcestershire sauce

5 drops Tabasco sauce

black pepper

My husband Larry (aka Lorenzo), doesn't do too much cooking, except for his famous tuna salad, but he does venture into the kitchen to make the best Bloody Mary. To get this recipe down on paper, I had to hold measuring spoons over the glass so as not to interfere with his creativity!

Pour vodka over ice in a 10-ounce glass. Add tomato juice, lemon juice, horseradish, Worcestershire and Tabasco. Stir to combine. Add several grindings of fresh black pepper. Serves 1.

CURLY LETTUCE SALAD WITH GRUYÈRE AND WALNUTS

6 cups fresh greens
¾ cup walnut halves
4 ounces Gruyère cheese, cut into ¼-inch cubes

VINAIGRETTE:

3 tablespoons red wine vinegar
9 tablespoons olive oil

1 teaspoon Dijon mustard
black pepper to taste

In a bowl combine greens, walnuts, and cheese.

In a screw-top jar combine vinegar, olive oil, Dijon, and pepper. Toss with greens.

CARAMEL BANANAS

9 tablespoons butter
6 tablespoons sugar
6 bananas, halved lengthwise
½ cup orange juice
1 tablespoon grated orange zest
6 tablespoons Myers's dark rum
1½ pints vanilla ice cream

In a large skillet melt butter. Add sugar and cook over low heat for 5 minutes, until sugar begins to color. Add bananas, cut side down, and cook, turning once, until almost tender (about 3 to 5 minutes). Remove bananas from pan.

Add orange juice and zest and shake pan to deglaze caramel. Add rum, heat briefly, and ignite, averting your face, or boil rum for several minutes to evaporate alcohol. Spoon flaming sauce over bananas and serve with a scoop of ice cream.

CHICKEN TIPS...

1. *When roasting a whole chicken, instead of using a fork, insert a wooden spoon into the cavity to help turn the bird over and prevent the juices from running out.*
2. *If you don't have leftover cooked chicken to use in chicken potpie, save time by poaching chicken breasts instead of a whole chicken. Or go to the local deli and buy cooked chicken in one piece.*
3. *Use unwaxed dental floss to truss a chicken the next time you run out of kitchen string.*

*T*his chicken dish was a star seller when I had my catering business. The recipe is easy to prepare, can be done ahead, and some might even say it can be frozen. I've made this dish for as few as 2 and as many as 100. You just keep preparing it in as many batches as you need. The entire menu can be made the day before, if desired, and reheated. If you do that, be sure to undercook the chicken and carrots slightly. The frozen oranges may be prepared several days ahead of time. Advance preparation will give you plenty of time the day of the party to set the table and put the finishing touches on the flowers.

THE PERFECT MAKE AHEAD DINNER PARTY

MENU

ICY BROCCOLI SOUP

CHICKEN VERONIQUE

GREEN RICE

SKILLET CARROTS

FROZEN ORANGES

BEVERAGE: DRY, MEDIUM-BODIED WHITE WINE

Icy Broccoli Soup

This soup is equally good hot or cold.

2 bunches broccoli
2 yellow onions, thinly
   sliced
4 cups chicken stock
salt and pepper to taste
pinch grated nutmeg
½–1 cup plain yogurt

Remove broccoli florets. Peel stems and cut into slices ¼ inch thick. Place all broccoli and onions in a 2-quart saucepan. Add stock, salt and pepper, and nutmeg. Bring to the boil. Reduce to simmering, cover, and cook until vegetables are soft, 15 to 20 minutes. Puree in 2 batches in a food processor fitted with a steel blade. Return to saucepan. Stir in enough yogurt until desired consistency. Adjust seasonings. Chill.

To dress soup up for company, garnish each serving with some additional blanched florets.

Chicken Veronique

3 whole skinless,
   boneless chicken
   breasts, halved
¼ teaspoon salt
¼ teaspoon black
   pepper
½ teaspoon dried
   tarragon
1 cup bread crumbs
8 tablespoons butter
¼ cup finely chopped
   onion
½ cup chicken stock
½ cup dry white wine
¾ pound green seedless
   grapes (about 2
   cups)
½ pound mushrooms,
   sliced

Preheat oven to 375°.

Sprinkle chicken breasts with salt, pepper, and tarragon, and coat with bread crumbs. In a large skillet melt 3 tablespoons butter and lightly brown chicken on both sides. You might have to do this in several batches. Remove to a heatproof shallow dish. Set aside.

Melt 3 tablespoons butter in same skillet. Add onion and sauté for 3 to 5 minutes, or until soft. Add chicken stock, wine, and grapes and bring to the boil. Using a wooden spoon, scrape skillet to dislodge any browned particles. Pour contents of skillet over chicken and bake, uncovered, for 30 minutes.

Melt remaining 2 tablespoons butter in skillet and sauté mushrooms. Pour over chicken and bake for 10 minutes more.

Green Rice

To save time, use a boxed pilaf that you just add liquid to.

Preheat oven to 350°.

Melt butter in a 1½-quart casserole. Add onion and cook for 5 minutes. Add rice and stir to coat with butter. Pour in stock, stir, and bring to the boil. Add salt, pepper, and thyme. Reduce to a simmer and put in oven. Cook for 18 minutes, or until liquid has been absorbed. You may set aside, covered, for 20 minutes. Stir in parsley before serving.

N O T E : *If necessary, this can be cooked on top of the stove to save oven space.*

4 tablespoons butter
¼ cup minced onion
1½ cups rice
3 cups boiling chicken
    stock
salt and pepper to taste
pinch dried thyme
¾ cup minced fresh
    parsley

Skillet Carrots

Place carrots, butter, and brown sugar in a skillet. Add enough water to just cover carrots. Cover skillet and bring to the boil. Cook at a low boil for 10 to 15 minutes, until tender and most of liquid has evaporated.

1½ pounds carrots, cut
    diagonally into ½-
    inch pieces (about
    5½ cups)
4 tablespoons butter
3 tablespoons brown
    sugar

Frozen Oranges

Slice oranges in half crosswise. Using a grapefruit knife, remove pulp and reserve for another use. Freeze shells overnight. Fill with sherbet, mounding the top slightly. Freeze until serving time. Garnish with fresh mint.

Variation: The same may be done with hollowed-out lemons filled with lemon sherbet, cassis ice, blueberry ice cream, and so on.

3 very large navel
    oranges
1 quart raspberry
    sherbet
fresh mint

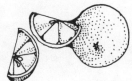

*O*N COOKING VEGETABLES...

1. *Vegetable cooking times vary, depending on the thickness of the slice. When you are in a big hurry, slice produce thinner to hasten the cooking time.*
2. *Vegetables can be sliced and blanched the day before the party. Run under cold water to prevent further cooking. Dry well and store in airtight plastic bags.*

*O*N REHEATING RICE...

1. *Rice may be cooked the day before. To reheat, bring to room temperature and add a little water to keep the rice from sticking to the bottom of the saucepan. Gently reheat, covered.*
2. *Reheat in the microwave in a covered casserole on* HIGH *for 2 to 3 minutes, stirring once.*

*E*NTERTAINING THOUGHTS

This is how to create one of my favorite table settings: Arrange about six chunky white candles in a zigzag fashion down the center of your dinner table and set pears around the candles. Add snippets of boxwood to fill in the gaps, and place pieces of gold ribbon decoratively around. I also like to tie some gold ribbon around the napkins and use 14-inch round gold doilies as place mats. Quite elegant!

MENU

ASPARAGUS
BUNDLES

MUSTARD CHICKEN

GRATED ZUCCHINI
AND CARROTS

SCALLOPED
POTATOES

STRAWBERRY COUPE
WITH GAUFRETTES

BEVERAGE:
CHILLED DRY ROSÉ

*T*his chicken dish is quite versatile in that it can be used as an hors d'oeuvre or as a main course. By removing the skin from the chicken before using, it becomes quite healthy fare. The chicken can be started in the morning and the vegetables precut. The recipes for Mustard Chicken and Strawberry Coupe come from Sally Figdor, a great friend and a great cook!

ASPARAGUS BUNDLES

3 dozen thin asparagus
12 slices provolone
cheese

VINAIGRETTE:

1 tablespoon minced
shallots
salt and pepper to taste
4 tablespoons red wine
vinegar
12 tablespoons olive oil
2 tablespoons minced
fresh parsley

Bring to the boil a pot of salted water large enough to hold asparagus. Peel stems of asparagus using a vegetable peeler or a sharp knife and trim spears to 6 inches long. Tie asparagus in 3 bundles with kitchen string. Drop in boiling salted water to blanch. They should still be slightly crunchy. Drain and run under cold water to cool. Dry on paper towels. Roll 1 piece of cheese around 3 spears, leaving tips exposed. Set aside.

Prepare vinaigrette. In a bowl whisk together shallots, salt and pepper, and red wine vinegar. Slowly whisk in olive oil and add parsley.

Arrange 2 bundles on a plate and drizzle vinaigrette on top.

MUSTARD CHICKEN

8 ounces Dijon mustard
4 tablespoons orange
marmalade
1 teaspoon dried basil
1½ tablespoons
vegetable oil
3 whole chicken
breasts, boned but
with skin left on

In a bowl combine Dijon, marmalade, and basil. Set aside ¼ cup. Add vegetable oil to remaining mixture in bowl and add chicken. Coat with marinade and refrigerate for 30 minutes, or longer if time permits.

Preheat oven to 350°. Arrange chicken in shallow baking dish and bake for 30 minutes, or until done. (You may set briefly under broiler to brown top.)

Serve with reserved sauce.

Variations:
1. Remove breasts from marinade, roll in bread crumbs, and sauté in skillet for 3 to 4 minutes per side.
2. Cut chicken into 1-inch cubes before marinating. Bake for 10 minutes and serve with toothpicks as an hors d'oeuvre with reserved sauce for dipping.

GRATED ZUCCHINI AND CARROTS

Grate carrots and zucchini in a food processor fitted with medium shredding blade to make long strands.

In a large skillet heat olive oil and garlic, being careful not to burn garlic. Add vegetables, oregano, salt and pepper. Toss quickly to coat with oil and cook for 5 minutes, or until vegetables are softened and heated through.

3 carrots, peeled
3 medium zucchini
3 tablespoons olive oil
1 clove garlic, crushed
1 teaspoon dried
    oregano
salt and pepper to taste

SCALLOPED POTATOES

Preheat oven to 425°. Grease a 10-inch oval baking dish, 2 inches deep.

By hand or in a food processor slice potatoes ⅛ inch thick. Arrange half of potatoes with slices overlapping in baking dish. Dot with 2 tablespoons butter and season with salt and pepper. Continue with remaining potatoes, 2 tablespoons butter, salt and pepper. Pour on enough milk to barely cover potatoes. Bake for 30 minutes, or until milk has been absorbed and potatoes start to get crispy.

Variation: Between the potato layers add a layer of ½ cup thinly sliced onions that have been sautéed in butter.

2 pounds boiling
    potatoes, peeled
4 tablespoons butter
salt and pepper to taste
2 cups boiling milk

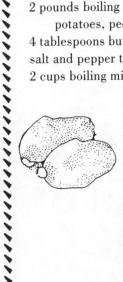

STRAWBERRY COUPE WITH GAUFRETTES

3 pints strawberries, washed, dried, and hulled
¼ cup Grand Marnier
1 cup heavy cream
1 tablespoon sifted confectioners' sugar
6 gaufrettes (fan-shaped cookies)

Cut the berries into quarters and place in a bowl with Grand Marnier. Refrigerate.

In bowl of an electric mixer whip heavy cream until soft peaks begin to form. Add sugar, approximately ¼ cup of drained strawberries, and 1 tablespoon Grand Marnier. Mix briefly to combine.

Spoon remaining strawberries into parfait glasses and top with whipped cream. Arrange a gaufrette to stand up in whipped cream.

ENTERTAINING THOUGHTS

If you choose your foods according to what's in season, you can't go wrong on freshness. Also, it's the most economical way to buy. A number of foods are in the market all the time, but produce is cheapest when it is that food's peak season.

Spring produce are:

Asparagus
Rhubarb
Morels
Fiddlehead ferns
Artichokes
Avocados
Belgian endive

Tender baby salad greens
Sorrel
Spinach
Vidalia onions
Strawberries
Lamb

EASY CHICKEN DINNER FOR FRIENDS

M E N U

STUFFED
MUSHROOM SALAD

CHICKEN MADEIRA

NUTTY WILD RICE

STEAMED BROCCOLI

APPLE TORTE

BEVERAGE:
DRY, MEDIUM-
BODIED WHITE WINE

The chicken can be assembled, but not baked, in the morning. Bring to room temperature before baking. Pop the apple torte in the oven before you get dressed for the evening and it will still be warm at serving time.

STUFFED MUSHROOM SALAD

18 medium to large
    fresh mushrooms
4 tablespoons butter
6 tablespoons finely
    chopped green onions
3 ounces blue cheese,
    crumbled
1 tablespoon bread crumbs
2 tablespoons chopped
    toasted walnuts
salt and pepper to taste

VINAIGRETTE:

1 tablespoon sherry
    vinegar
2 tablespoons wine
    vinegar
9 tablespoons olive oil
salt and pepper to taste

3 cups red leaf lettuce
3 cups Bibb lettuce
chives or chive blossoms

Preheat oven to 350°.

Remove stems from mushrooms and finely chop. Set aside caps. In a saucepan melt butter and add green onions and chopped mushrooms. Sauté until tender. Remove from heat. Stir in blue cheese, bread crumbs, walnuts, and salt and pepper. Spoon mixture into mushroom caps. (This may be done the day before and refrigerated. Bring to room temperature before baking.) Bake for 12 minutes.

In a screw-top jar combine vinegars, olive oil, and salt and pepper.

While baking, toss salad greens with vinaigrette. Put on individual plates and arrange 3 mushroom caps on top of each serving. Garnish with chives and/or chive blossoms.

CHICKEN MADEIRA

½ cup bread crumbs
½ cup flour
1 teaspoon salt
⅛ teaspoon black
    pepper
⅛ teaspoon paprika
½ teaspoon dried
    oregano
6 skinless, boneless
    chicken breast halves
4 tablespoons butter
2 tablespoons vegetable oil
1 cup Madeira

Preheat oven to 350°. Grease a shallow baking dish.

On a large sheet of wax paper combine bread crumbs, flour, salt, pepper, paprika, and oregano. Dredge chicken in this mixture. Press crumbs with fingers to adhere.

In a large skillet melt 1 tablespoon butter with oil. Sauté chicken on both sides quickly until lightly browned. Remove chicken to a baking dish. Melt remaining 3 tablespoons butter in skillet and add Madeira. Bring to the boil and scrape up browned bits clinging to pan. Pour over chicken and bake for 30 minutes.

N O T E : *If you need your oven for another dish, the chicken can be cooked in a skillet on top of the stove or made ahead, undercooked slightly, and reheated.*

Nutty wild rice

Preheat oven to 350°.

Toast pecans on a cookie sheet for 5 minutes. Coarsely chop and set aside.

In a 1½-quart saucepan bring stock to the boil. Add rice and butter and cook, covered, at a simmer for 1 hour, or until rice is tender and stock is absorbed. Add pecans to rice with salt and pepper to taste.

½ cup pecan halves
3 cups chicken stock
1½ cups wild rice
3 tablespoons butter
salt and pepper to taste

On toasting shelled nuts...

Preheat oven to 350°. Spread nuts on a baking sheet and toast about 5 minutes. They should brown lightly, but not burn. Toasting helps bring out a fuller flavor.

Apple torte

This recipe comes from Barbara Schlein, a friend who has a business called Delicious Designs, baking fabulous custom-sculpted cakes.

½ cup butter, softened
1 cup sugar
1 cup sifted flour
1 teaspoon baking
    powder
pinch salt
2 eggs
2 apples, cored, peeled,
    and sliced into
    eighths
¼ teaspoon ground
    cinnamon mixed
    with ½ teaspoon
    sugar

N O T E : *This dessert freezes beautifully. When completely cool, wrap well and freeze. Defrost and heat in 350° oven for several minutes.*

Preheat oven to 350°. Grease a 9-inch springform pan. Line bottom with a piece of wax paper and grease also.

In the bowl of an electric mixer cream together butter and sugar. When fluffy, add, all at once, flour, baking powder, salt, and eggs. Beat well to combine. Batter will be slightly thick.

Spoon batter into prepared pan and smooth top. Arrange apples in circular fashion on top of batter. Sprinkle with cinnamon-sugar mixture. Bake on middle rack of oven for 1 hour. When done it should be golden brown. Release sides of pan and set on wire rack to cool.

Variations:
1. Substitute 12 purple plums, skinned, pitted, and cut in half for apples. Arrange on top, rounded side up. Sprinkle with lemon juice, cinnamon, and sugar.
2. Substitute 6 ounces chocolate chips for apples. Sprinkle with sugar and reduce baking time to 35 minutes.

Some apple advice...

1. *Note these helpful equivalents when baking:*
   3 medium apples = 1 pound; 1 pound unpeeled apples = 3 cups peeled, sliced fruit; 2–3 pounds apples = 9-inch pie
2. *Carbon steel knives cause apples to turn brown. Be sure to use stainless steel.*
3. *The varieties of apples are endless so I like to remember the best one for each category of eating and cooking: The Granny Smith is the best all-purpose apple. The Cortland is a good salad apple because it doesn't turn brown too quickly. The Rome Beauty is best for baked apples. And the Rhode Island Greening is excellent for making pies.*

My husband Larry's all-time favorite dinner is turkey. I used to cook the vegetables ahead, make turkey stock with the bones, and thicken the stock for gravy. The meal tasted wonderful, but it took a considerable amount of time, which meant I didn't make it that often.

Having less time these days, I have shortened my method of preparation quite a bit, but with even better results. Once the turkey is popped in the oven, it might take a while to cook, but you don't have to be chained to the stove. Put the bird in the oven 1 hour before your guests arrive and let it finish cooking during the cocktail hour.

The gravy is easier and

E-Z TURKEY DINNER

MENU

E-Z ROAST TURKEY BREAST

KASHA WITH MUSHROOMS

CRANBERRY SAUCE

STRING BEANS WITH FRIZZY ONIONS

BAKED APPLES WITH CURRANTS

BEVERAGE: ROBUST, VERY FULL-BODIED RED WINE

healthier with pureed cooked vegetables being used as the thickening agent. If you choose to make this on Sunday for 2, you end up with turkey to freeze in smaller amounts to use for hash, turkey potpie, etcetera, and the carcass to use for soup. Instead of using canned cranberry sauce, freshly made sauce is often found in gourmet shops and sold by the pound.

E-Z ROAST TURKEY BREAST

3 carrots, sliced
1 onion, sliced
1 bunch thyme
5–6 pound turkey breast
salt to taste
2 tablespoons butter,
    softened
vegetable oil
½–1 cup chicken stock

Preheat oven to 325°.

In roasting pan place carrots, onion, and half of thyme. Turn turkey, breast side down, sprinkle with salt, and stuff with remaining thyme. Place breast side up in pan on top of vegetables. Rub with butter. Dip a piece of cheesecloth, large enough to cover turkey, in a shallow dish filled with vegetable oil. When cheesecloth is moistened, drape over turkey breast. (At this point turkey may be refrigerated overnight, covered. Bring to room temperature before cooking.)

Roast for about 2 hours, or until turkey reaches 175° on thermometer, basting occasionally with juices in pan. Remove turkey from oven and let stand for 20 minutes before carving.

KASHA WITH MUSHROOMS

2 tablespoons butter
½ cup chopped onions
½ pound mushrooms,
    sliced
2 cups chicken stock
1 cup kasha
1 egg, beaten
salt and pepper to taste

In a skillet melt butter and sauté onions and mushrooms until softened. Add stock and simmer briefly. Set aside.
In another skillet combine kasha and egg and then cook, stirring constantly, for 3 minutes, or until grains separate. Pour stock mixture in, add salt and pepper. Bring to the boil. Cover, lower heat, and simmer for 15 minutes, or until liquid is absorbed.

STRING BEANS WITH FRIZZY ONIONS

Bring a large pot of salted water to the boil. Add beans, return to the boil, and cook uncovered for about 8 minutes. Taste to test for desired doneness. Drain.

Melt butter in a skillet and sauté green onions until brown and crispy. Toss beans with frizzy onions.

2½ pounds string beans, trimmed
2 tablespoons butter
1 bunch green onions, thinly sliced

BAKED APPLES WITH CURRANTS

Preheat oven to 350°. Grease a shallow baking dish.

Slice a piece from the bottom of each apple so it will sit firmly upright in baking dish. Core each apple, being careful not to pierce through to bottom. Enlarge the core opening to be able to hold filling.

In a bowl combine brown sugar, butter, walnuts, currants or raisins, and zest. Stuff each apple with a portion of filling and place a cinnamon stick in center. Bake for 30 minutes, or until soft.

6 apples (Cortland or Rome Beauty)
½ cup brown sugar
3 tablespoons butter, melted
¼ cup chopped walnuts
¼ cup currants or raisins
1 teaspoon lemon zest
6 cinnamon sticks

MORE APPLE FACTS...

1. *When making pastry crusts for apple pies, substitute cold cider for the water called for in the piecrust recipes for extra apple flavor.*
2. *For a more interesting flavor, use two or three different types of apples when making applesauce.*
3. *When making scalloped potatoes, use half apple slices and half potatoes for a change.*
4. *Use apple cider as the liquid when making baked apples.*
5. *Boil apples in water to give a fresh scent to a newly opened, musty house.*

SUPREME CHICKEN SOUP ০০০০০০০০০০০০০

If you want to add a soup course to this menu, this recipe can't be beat. It's hard to believe that it is made with canned chicken broth. There is no compromise on quality here—it is the best and easiest chicken soup.

1 46-ounce can College Inn chicken broth
5¾ cups water
1 small parsnip, sliced ⅛ inch thick
1 stalk celery, halved

2 carrots, sliced ⅛ inch thick
1 green onion, halved
1 clove garlic
1 small parsley root (including greens)

white pepper to taste
pinch paprika
1 boneless, skinless chicken breast
2 tablespoons chopped fresh dill

In a large pot bring all ingredients (except chicken breast, carrots and dill) to the boil. Reduce to simmering. Add chicken breast and carrots and simmer for 45 minutes to 1 hour, adding dill 5 minutes before finished cooking. (Remove chicken breast after 20 minutes and reserve for another use.)

Remove and discard celery, green onion, garlic, and parsley root. Adjust seasoning and serve. *Makes 10 cups.*

ENTERTAINING THOUGHTS

When autumn arrives, there is a certain crispness in the air and our thoughts turn to entirely different foods from summer. Look for some of these:

Winter squash — *Pears*
Brussels sprouts — *Pumpkins*
Cabbage — *Cranberries*
Cauliflower — *Kumquats*
Celeriac — *Pomegranates*
Wild mushrooms — *Persimmons*
Truffles — *Apple cider*
Chestnuts — *Beaujolais Nouveau*
Apples — *Oysters*

VEAL

NO-OVEN DINNER

MENU

TOP-OF-THE-STOVE
LOIN OF VEAL WITH
WILD MUSHROOM
SAUCE ▲▲▲▲▲

MINTED CARROT
PUREE ▮▮▮▮▮▮▮

RICE CAKES • • •

CHOCOLATE VELVET ∿∿

DAINTY COOKIES ▪▪▪▪▪▪

BEVERAGE:
DRY FULL-BODIED
WHITE WINE ◢◢◢◢

*S*ometimes there isn't enough room in the oven to cook all the dishes needed for a dinner party. This veal dish is cooked on top of the stove, leaving your oven free for the side dishes.
The carrot puree, rice cakes, and chocolate velvet can be made ahead.

TOP-OF-THE-STOVE LOIN OF VEAL WITH WILD MUSHROOM SAUCE

VEAL:

3–4 pounds loin of veal,
  boned and tied
3 tablespoons olive oil
1½ tablespoons dried
  rosemary or
  tarragon
black pepper to taste
2 cloves garlic, minced
5 slices bacon
2 tablespoons butter
½ cup dry white wine
½ cup water

Rub veal all over with 1 tablespoon oil, rosemary or tarragon, pepper, and garlic. Arrange bacon slices over veal and hold in place with toothpicks. In a deep sauté pan, heat butter and remaining 2 tablespoons oil and add veal. Sauté on all sides until brown, about 4 minutes per side. Add wine and water and reduce heat to low. Cover and cook for 1½ to 2 hours, basting 2 or 3 times with pan juices. The roast is done at a thermometer reading of 175°. Reserve 2 tablespoons of pan juices to add to sauce.

WILD MUSHROOM SAUCE:

3 tablespoons butter
¼ pound fresh wild
  mushrooms (such
  as cepes, shiitake,
  or porcini), coarsely
  chopped
½ pound fresh
  mushrooms,
  coarsely chopped
salt and pepper to taste
¾ cup heavy cream
1 tablespoon minced
  fresh parsley
1 tablespoon minced
  fresh tarragon, or
  1½ teaspoons dried

While the veal is cooking, melt butter in a skillet and add mushrooms, salt, and pepper. Sauté until liquid has evaporated, about 5 minutes. Add cream, parsley, and tarragon. Bring almost to the boil, lower heat, and simmer for about 15 minutes, or until sauce is slightly reduced and thickened. Add 2 tablespoons of reserved pan juices to sauce.

Remove strings and bacon. Slice veal and serve with sauce.

Minted Carrot Puree

In a large pot bring salted water to the boil. Add carrots and mint and cook for 20 minutes, or until carrots are soft. Drain. In a food processor puree carrots with cream, sugar, and salt and pepper until smooth. Sprinkle with parsley and serve.

3 cups salted water
1½ pounds carrots, peeled, cut into 1-inch pieces
1 teaspoon chopped fresh mint
¾ cup heavy cream
3 tablespoons butter, softened
1 teaspoon sugar
salt and pepper to taste
1 tablespoon minced fresh parsley

N O T E : *May be prepared ahead and gently reheated in double boiler.*

Rice Cakes

The next time you have rice pilaf, risotto, or just plain rice left over, save it to make rice cakes for your next night's dinner.

Place rice and Parmesan in a bowl and add eggs, salt and pepper, and parsley. Form into 2-inch cakes.

In a 10-inch heavy skillet melt butter and olive oil together over moderately high heat. When hot, add cakes and use a spatula to flatten. Cook over moderate heat until crisp, about 2 minutes. Turn and cook for another 30 seconds to 1 minute. *Makes 18.*

2 cups cooked rice, cooled
⅓ cup grated Parmesan cheese
2 eggs, lightly beaten
salt and pepper to taste
2 tablespoons minced fresh parsley
2 tablespoons butter
1 tablespoon olive oil

N O T E : *Rice cakes can be prepared ahead and reheated on a cookie sheet in a 375° oven for about 5 minutes.*

CHOCOLATE VELVET

1 6-ounce package
    chocolate chips
3 eggs, separated
¼ cup water
pinch salt
⅓ cup brown sugar
garnish: whipped
    cream, chocolate
    shavings

Melt chocolate chips in top of double boiler. Lightly beat egg yolks until lemon colored, add to chips, and beat well. Add water and beat until smooth.

In the bowl of an electric mixer beat egg whites with salt until peaks begin to form. Slowly beat in brown sugar. Fold egg white mixture into chocolate mixture. Spoon into parfait glasses and chill until serving time. Garnish with a dollop of whipped cream and chocolate shavings.

Serve with dainty cookies.

ON CRYSTAL STAINS...

To remove stubborn stains from a crystal decanter (especially one with a narrow neck), fill the decanter with a solution of half water and half white vinegar. Set aside to soak. If the stain is particularly difficult, add some fine sand or powdered denture cleaner to the vinegar mixture.

ENTERTAINING THOUGHTS

When I first got married, I ruined more tablecloths than I care to think about because I didn't know how to remove wine stains.

1. *Deal with the problem as soon as possible after your guests have left. I feel that making a project out of it immediately, in front of the guilty party, just makes that person feel even more uncomfortable.*
2. *Blot up excess liquid. Then rinse out as much of the stain as you can with warm tap water.*
3. *You might try club soda or a 50/50 solution of white vinegar and water.*
4. *If all else fails, take a trip to the dry cleaner.*

New Twist on Old-Fashioned Dinner

MENU

VEAL MEAT LOAF

BRAISED SPINACH

MASHED SWEET
POTATOES

CHOCOLATE MINT
CHIP BROWNIES

BEVERAGE:
RICH, FULL-BODIED
RED WINE

*F*ive years ago, if you invited
friends over for dinner and
served them meat loaf and
mashed potatoes, tongues
would surely have been
wagging! Then the all-
American meat loaf became the
rage. This dinner is a new twist
on the old-fashioned meat loaf
and mashed potatoes dinner.
The meat loaf is made with
veal instead of beef, the
mashed potatoes are made with
sweet potatoes, and the ever
popular chocolate brownies are
made with mint chocolate
morsels.
All but the meat loaf can be

*prepared and cooked the day before, and brought to room
temperature before reheating. The spinach and sweet potatoes
can be reheated while the meat loaf bakes.*

Veal meat loaf

2 tablespoons butter
½ cup minced onions
2 medium tomatoes,
    chopped
1 clove garlic, minced
¼ teaspoon salt
1 teaspoon dried thyme
1 cup bread crumbs
½ cup milk
1 pound ground veal
black pepper to taste
3 tablespoons minced
    fresh parsley
1 egg

Preheat oven to 350°. Grease a 9″-x-5″-x-2½″ loaf pan.

In a skillet melt butter and sauté onions for 5 minutes.
Add tomatoes, garlic, salt, and thyme. Cover and cook
on medium heat for 5 minutes. Uncover, raise heat,
and cook until most of liquid has evaporated. Put in a
mixing bowl.

Soak bread crumbs in milk for 5 minutes and then
squeeze out as much milk as possible. Add bread
crumbs to bowl with meat, pepper, parsley, and egg.
Stir to combine.

Pack mixture into loaf pan and bake for 45 minutes to
1 hour, or until meat thermometer reads 175°.

Variation: The meat loaf recipe can also be formed into
patties and cooked in a skillet. You can get the food on
the table faster, but it requires more of your attention.

Form the meat mixture into 6 patties, ½ inch thick.
Just before sautéing, dredge in flour, shaking off excess. Melt 2 tablespoons butter with 1 tablespoon vegetable oil in a large skillet over moderately high heat.
Add patties and brown for 2 to 3 minutes on each side.
Lower heat to moderate, cover, and cook for 15 minutes, turning once.

Braised Spinach

Put spinach in a large heavy saucepan and don't add water. Cover and steam on medium heat until wilted, about 5 minutes. Stir occasionally. Remove and coarsely chop. Return to saucepan with butter, salt and pepper, and nutmeg. Cover and cook slowly, about 10 minutes, until spinach has absorbed butter.

N O T E : *May be prepared ahead and reheated.*

3 pounds fresh spinach,
   washed but not
   dried
4 tablespoons butter
salt and pepper to taste
pinch grated nutmeg

Mashed Sweet Potatoes

Scrape out flesh of sweet potatoes and mash with butter (or put through food mill). Beat in with whisk crème fraîche, bourbon, salt and pepper, and nutmeg until fluffy.

N O T E : *May be reheated, covered, in 350° oven for 20 minutes.*

3 pounds sweet
   potatoes, cooked
6 tablespoons butter,
   softened
¼ to ½ cup crème fraîche
1½ tablespoons bourbon
salt and pepper to taste
grated nutmeg to taste

Chocolate Mint Chip Brownies

Preheat oven to 350°. Grease a 9″-x-13″ pan.

In a saucepan melt butter and chocolate squares. When smooth, set aside to cool completely.

In the bowl of an electric mixer beat eggs with salt until foamy. Slowly add sugar and then vanilla. Fold in chocolate mixture. Before thoroughly combined, fold in flour. Stir in morsels and walnuts. Pour batter into pan and bake for 25 minutes. Cool and cut into squares.

1 stick (½ cup) butter
5 ounces unsweetened
   chocolate squares
4 eggs, room
   temperature
¼ teaspoon salt
1½ cups sugar
1 teaspoon vanilla
   extract
1 cup sifted flour
½ cup semisweet mint
   chocolate morsels
½ cup coarsely chopped
   walnuts

QUICK-COOK SWEET POTATOES . . .

Place sweet potatoes in microwave 4 at a time. Pierce skins and arrange in a circle, on a paper towel, 1 inch apart. Cook on HIGH for 10 to 13 minutes, or until tender. Let stand for 5 to 10 minutes.

If cooking conventionally, bake in 400° oven for about 40 minutes.

HOMEMADE CRÈME FRAÎCHE . . .

Crème fraîche is more widely available than it used to be but, if you can't find it, take heart. You don't have to do without. Here's how to make it yourself:

Add 1 tablespoon buttermilk to 1 cup heavy cream. Stir to combine and leave out at room temperature, covered, for 8 hours, or overnight, until it has thickened. Then refrigerate. It will keep for about 10 days.

LAMB

SHOW-OFF
DINNER

MENU

HERBED RACK OF
LAMB   ●●●●●

PRALINE CARROT
PUREE   +++++

SAUTÉED POTATOES
AND ONIONS   ▲▲▲▲▲

SOUSED ORANGES
AND RASPBERRIES   ▼▼▼

FLORENTINE
COOKIES   ▪▪▪▪▪▪

BEVERAGE:
RICH, FULL-BODIED   ○ ○ ○
RED WINE

*T*his dinner
will show you off
to be an excellent hostess—and
it takes only a minimum
amount of effort! The rack of
lamb can be assembled ahead
of time, as well as the carrot
puree and Joni Muskovitz's
soused oranges and
raspberries.

HERBED RACK OF LAMB

2 racks of lamb,
   trimmed (see Note)
2 tablespoons olive oil
2 tablespoons mixed
   dried herbs (choose
   from rosemary,
   tarragon, and sage)

Wrap exposed chop bones in aluminum foil. Brush lamb with olive oil and sprinkle herbs on top, pressing in with fingertips. Let marinate for 30 minutes to overnight.

Preheat oven to 500°. Place racks in roasting pan fat side down and roast for 20 minutes. Reduce heat to 400°, turn over, and roast for 15 minutes more.

N O T E : *Have butcher French-cut the racks, exposing the bone.*

PRALINE CARROT PUREE

1½ pounds carrots,
   peeled, sliced
   ¼ inch thick
¾ cup heavy cream
6 tablespoons butter,
   softened
1 teaspoon white sugar
salt and pepper to taste
¼ cup brown sugar
½ cup chopped pecans

Preheat oven to 350°. Grease a casserole.

In a saucepan boil carrots in salted water for 10 minutes, or until tender. Drain and puree in food processor fitted with a steel blade. Add to puree heavy cream, 3 tablespoons butter, white sugar, and salt and pepper; process to combine.

Transfer to casserole. Sprinkle top with brown sugar and pecans. (May be made ahead to this point.) Dot with remaining 3 tablespoons butter and bake for 20 minutes, or until top is lightly browned.

SAUTÉED POTATOES AND ONIONS

⅔ cup olive oil
1½ pounds red onions,
   thinly sliced
1½ pounds red
   potatoes, thinly
   sliced
salt and pepper to taste
6 sprigs fresh thyme

Heat ⅓ cup olive oil in a large heavy skillet and sauté onions slowly until lightly browned, about 15 minutes. Set aside.

Meanwhile, soak potato slices in a bowl of cold water. Drain and change the water 2 more times to remove starch. Drain and dry well.

Add remaining ⅓ cup oil to skillet and when hot add potatoes, salt and pepper, and thyme. Using a spatula, turn potatoes so they brown. When well browned on both sides, return onions to pan and mix with potatoes before serving.

SOUSED ORANGES AND RASPBERRIES

Using a sharp knife, peel oranges, removing white pith. Slice ¼ inch thick and put in a glass bowl. Add sugar and Grand Marnier. Refrigerate for 1 hour.

To serve, arrange some oranges on each dessert plate in circular fashion and top with raspberries. Sprinkle on liquid mixture from oranges.

6 navel oranges
2 tablespoons sugar
3 tablespoons Grand
   Marnier
1 pint raspberries

NO-RECIPE-NEEDED HORS D'OEUVRES...

Here are some easy yet elegant suggestions:

- *room temperature tortellini tossed with pesto and threaded on a skewer*
- *curried mayonnaise on a cracker, topped with sliced egg and capers*
- *sliced French bread toasted, rubbed with garlic, and topped with chopped tomatoes, basil, salt, pepper, and a little olive oil*
- *endive leaves filled with Boursin cheese and a sprig of watercress*
- *toast topped with a thin slice of onion, a dab of mayonnaise, and a sprinkling of Parmesan, and popped under the broiler*
- *bowls of cherry or pear tomatoes served with mixture of ½ sour cream, ½ mayonnaise, and curry powder to taste.*

ENTERTAINING THOUGHTS

If an heirloom set of silver napkin rings haven't been sent your way yet, consider some of these substitutes: bangle bracelets, hoop earrings, an individual flower atop each napkin, and grapevine twigs twisted in a circle.

WINTER SUNDAY SUPPER

MENU

STUFFED LAMB
CHOPS

ACORN SQUASH
PUREE

MUSHROOM BARLEY
CASSEROLE

YOGURT WITH
SMASHED BERRIES

SHORTBREAD
COOKIES

BEVERAGE:
RICH, FULL-BODIED
RED WINE

Some people traditionally serve leg of lamb every Sunday. For a change, try these stuffed lamb chops.

If you attack this menu in the right order you've got it made. Begin by cooking the squash. Then, marinate the berries and follow that with assembling the mushroom barley casserole to bake. While the casserole is baking, stuff the chops. This can all be done early in the day, and the squash puree and casserole can be reheated while the chops are cooking.

Stuffed lamb chops

I can't tell you how many times I have served main dishes and forgotten to remove the strings! It has become a standing joke in our house. I have found the best way to deal with mistakes is to laugh at them instead of trying to cover them up.

Preheat broiler.

Using a small knife, cut a pocket in the side of lamb chops. In a bowl mash together butter, chives, parsley, and mint. Pack butter mixture into pockets. Using kitchen string, wrap around chops 2 times to hold closed.

Grill or broil chops 4 inches from heat source for 8 to 10 minutes, or to desired doneness, turning once. Season with salt and pepper and remove strings before serving.

6 loin lamb chops, 1½ inches thick, trimmed of fat
1½ sticks (¾ cup) butter, softened
2 tablespoons minced fresh chives
2 tablespoons minced fresh parsley
2 tablespoons minced fresh mint
salt and pepper to taste

Acorn squash puree

This is one of my favorite side dishes since it adds a beautiful burst of color to the dinner plate, and better yet, it can be prepared ahead.

Preheat oven to 375°. Grease a baking sheet.

Halve squash lengthwise and remove seeds and fibers. Place cut side down on baking sheet and bake for 45 minutes, or until soft.

Scoop out flesh into the bowl of a food processor fitted with a steel blade. Add remaining ingredients and process.

N O T E : *This recipe may be reheated gently in a double boiler.*

4 pounds acorn squash
6 tablespoons butter, softened, cut into 6 pieces
2 tablespoons lime juice
1 tablespoon dark rum
1 teaspoon salt
black pepper to taste
grated zest of 1 lime

MUSHROOM BARLEY CASSEROLE

4 tablespoons butter
1 cup minced onions
1 small clove garlic,
    minced
1½ cups barley
½ pound mushrooms,
    thinly sliced
1 teaspoon dried
    tarragon
salt to taste
4½ cups beef stock

Preheat oven to 350°.

In a casserole melt butter. Add onions and garlic and cook for 5 minutes. Add barley and stir to coat with butter. Add mushrooms, tarragon, and salt. Cook for 2 minutes. Add stock and bring to the boil. Cover and bake for 1 hour, until barley is tender and liquid is absorbed.

Variation: Use wild mushrooms instead of domestic for a great flavor enhancer.

YOGURT WITH SMASHED BERRIES

1½ pints strawberries,
    washed and hulled
4 tablespoons Grand
    Marnier
4 8-ounce containers
    plain or vanilla
    yogurt

Set 6 perfect berries aside. In a bowl mash remaining strawberries with Grand Marnier and set aside to marinate.

When ready to serve, fold berries into yogurt and serve in stemmed glasses. Top dessert with reserved berries.

Serve with shortbread cookies.

ANOTHER MICROWAVE TIP...

To microwave squash, place one 1½-pound whole squash, pierced with a fork, on a paper towel in the oven. Cook on HIGH for 8 to 10 minutes, turning after 5 minutes. Let stand for 5 to 10 minutes. To cook 2 squash, microwave on HIGH for 12 to 15 minutes, turning once. Let stand for 5 to 10 minutes.

SOME SHORTBREAD SHORTCUTS...

Start out with store-bought shortbread and transform it into a variety of desserts:

1. *Roll in confectioners' sugar mixed with a blend of ground cinnamon and nutmeg.*
2. *Roll in cocoa.*
3. *Dip in melted caramels and then in chopped pecans.*
4. *Brush with honey and roll in sesame seeds.*

RAINY DAY PICNIC

MENU

CHILLED CARROT SOUP

LAMB PATTIES

HOMEMADE POTATO CHIPS

CHUTNEY

LEMON-APRICOT BUNDT CAKE

BEVERAGE: LEMONADE WITH MINT

When quick cooking is the order of the day, ground meat is the perfect choice. However, instead of beef, try ground lamb for a change. The recipes for the Chilled Carrot Soup and Lemon-Apricot Bundt Cake come from my friend Ellen Agress, one of the busiest working women I know. With 2 children and a fantastic job, she still manages to entertain beautifully. She served these recipes as part of a recent dinner party.

CARROT SOUP

2 tablespoons butter
2 medium yellow
    onions, chopped
2 pounds carrots,
    peeled, cut into
    ¼-inch-thick slices
2–3 cups chicken stock
8 ounces plain yogurt
1 cup milk
pinch cayenne pepper
salt to taste
3 tablespoons chopped
    fresh dill

In a saucepan melt butter. When hot, add onions and sauté for 3 minutes. Add carrots and 2 cups stock to pan. Bring to the boil, reduce heat to simmering, and cook for 20 minutes, or until vegetables are softened.

In a food processor fitted with a steel blade puree in batches, if necessary. Add yogurt and milk. Process to combine. Return to saucepan. Adjust soup's consistency by adding more stock or milk. Season with cayenne pepper, salt, and dill. Serve either hot or chilled.

LAMB PATTIES

2 pounds ground lean
    lamb
4 tablespoons butter
5 tablespoons minced
    onion
½ cup plus 2
    tablespoons bread
    crumbs
1½ eggs, lightly beaten
    (beat separately
    and add *half* the
    second egg)
5 tablespoons minced
    fresh parsley
salt and pepper to taste
½ cup flour
1 tablespoon vegetable
    oil
5 ounces red wine

Place lamb in a bowl. Melt 1 tablespoon butter in a skillet. Add onion and sauté until softened. Add onion to lamb along with bread crumbs, eggs, parsley, and salt and pepper. Shape into 6 patties. Roll patties lightly in flour, shaking off excess. Wipe out skillet and add 2 tablespoons butter and oil. When butter is hot, add patties and pan-fry for 3 to 4 minutes per side. Lamb patties should be slightly well done and not pink. Remove patties and keep warm while preparing the sauce.

Add red wine to skillet, turn heat to high, and boil rapidly, scraping up browned particles. Boil until mixture is almost syrupy. Turn off heat, add 1 tablespoon butter to sauce, and stir until incorporated. Pour over lamb and serve.

HOMEMADE POTATO CHIPS

Preheat oven to 450°.

Brush potato slices generously with butter. Arrange in a single layer on baking sheets (you will need to do 2 sheets at a time or bake in several batches) until crisp and browned, 15 to 20 minutes. Watch that the chips don't burn.

3 Idaho potatoes,
    peeled, sliced
    ⅛ inch thick
1 stick (½ cup) butter,
    melted

LEMON-APRICOT BUNDT CAKE

Preheat oven to 325°. Grease and lightly flour a bundt pan with a tube at least 4 or 5 inches high.

Place cake ingredients in the bowl of an electric mixer and beat for 10 minutes. Pour batter into pan leaving 2 inches below top of pan. Bake for 1 hour. Remove from oven and cool on rack for 5 minutes in pan. Invert pan and set cake aside on rack to cool completely.

In a bowl beat together the icing ingredients. When smooth, spread over top of cake and let glaze drip down sides. Garnish with coconut. *Serves 12.*

CAKE:

1 package Duncan
    Hines Lemon
    Supreme Cake Mix
¾ cup vegetable oil
1 5-ounce can apricot
    nectar
½ cup sugar
4 eggs
1 teaspoon lemon
    extract
grated rind of 1 lemon

ICING:

¾ cup confectioners'
    sugar
juice of 1 lemon
1 teaspoon Cointreau

GARNISH:

shredded coconut

ENTERTAINING THOUGHTS

Next time you have a picnic planned and it rains, don't call it off. Bring your picnic indoors and set out blankets on the floor!

S OUP HINT...

Sometimes I find it easier to do small chopping tasks by hand instead of in the food processor to avoid cleanup. Although, if you think ahead, for this soup you can chop the onions, remove; slice the carrots, remove; and puree the soup, only washing the food processor after performing 3 tasks.

M OM'S PITA CRISPS

These crisps are very versatile—and are positively addictive! They can be passed in a' basket to accompany a soup course, charcuterie, or salads. Also, they are terrific to munch on with drinks.

2 sticks (1 cup)
   butter, softened
½ teaspoon dried
   dill
½ teaspoon dried
   basil
5 rounds pita bread,
   split horizontally
3 tablespoons grated
   Parmesan cheese

Preheat oven to 375°.

In a food processor cream butter until smooth. Add dill and basil.

Lightly spread split pita rounds with butter mixture. Sprinkle Parmesan on top.

Cut rounds in half and then into 3 or 4 triangles. Place on a baking sheet in a single layer and bake until lightly browned, 3 to 5 minutes. Watch closely so they don't burn. Bake in several batches.

These may be frozen in plastic bags and reheated straight from the freezer. *Makes 60 to 80 pieces.*

BEEF AND PORK

STEAK DINNER

MENU

My mother has made this steak recipe since I was a little girl. I'm not much of a meat eater, but this recipe is definitely special!
The soup and bananas can be prepared the day before. And the steak can be marinated overnight.

VICHYSSOISE WITH
RED PEPPER DICE

MOM'S SPECIAL
STEAK

CORN ON THE COB
WITH HERB BUTTER

GRILLED LEEKS

FROZEN
CHOCOLATE
BANANAS

BEVERAGE:
VODKA GIMLET

Vichyssoise with Red Pepper Dice

3 cups peeled, sliced
    potatoes
1½ cups sliced onions
1½ cups sliced leeks
    (white part only)
6 cups chicken stock
2 teaspoons salt
white pepper to taste
1 cup heavy cream
1 red bell pepper, finely
    diced

In a saucepan simmer potatoes, onions, leeks, chicken stock, salt and pepper, partially covered, for 40 minutes, or until vegetables are tender.

Puree in batches in a food processor fitted with a steel blade. Stir in heavy cream. Garnish with red pepper. Serve hot or cold.

Mom's Special Steak

2 garlic cloves, crushed
¾ cup soy sauce
6 tablespoons dark
    brown sugar
3 tablespoons olive oil
black pepper to taste
3 quarter-size discs
    fresh ginger
3 pounds sirloin steak,
    at least 1 inch thick

In a shallow dish combine all ingredients except steak. Add steak and set aside to marinate. (This may be assembled quickly in the morning and set aside in refrigerator to marinate all day.)

Bring to room temperature before cooking. Prepare coals for grilling.

Lightly oil the grill before placing steak on it. Once coals are hot, grill for at least 4 minutes on each side for rare, depending on thickness. Remove and slice. You can also broil in a preheated oven.

Grilled Leeks

12 small leeks, washed
    and trimmed
3 tablespoons Herb
    Butter (see
    following recipe),
    melted

Prepare coals for grilling.

Thread leeks on long skewers. Grill for 10 to 15 minutes, basting with herb butter. Turn leeks so they are evenly charred.

CORN ON THE COB WITH HERB BUTTER

In a bowl mash together butter, parsley, dill, and Tabasco. Set aside in a crock.

Bring large pot of water to the boil. Add corn, cover, and when water returns to the boil, remove from heat. Let stand in water for at least 5 minutes and up to 20 minutes.

Serve with herb butter.

HERB BUTTER:

1 stick (½ cup) butter, softened
1½ tablespoons minced fresh parsley
1½ tablespoons minced fresh dill
Tabasco sauce to taste

6 ears corn, shucked

FROZEN CHOCOLATE BANANAS

In a medium skillet melt butter and chocolate over low heat. Stir in evaporated milk. Remove from heat.

Peel bananas and insert a skewer into one end of each banana. Dip one at a time into chocolate to coat. Place on cookie sheet lined with wax paper and freeze. Remove from freezer 10 minutes before serving.

4 tablespoons butter
6 ounces semisweet chocolate morsels
3 tablespoons evaporated milk
6 bananas

CORN RELISH

I always like to cook extra corn to have leftovers to use in salad, corn muffins, pancakes, etc. The following recipe is one of my all-time favorites. Serve as a dip with peeled jícama cut into sticks, or with taco chips. It is also a wonderful side dish with, for example, grilled salmon.

In a medium bowl combine all ingredients. Use the back of a fork to mash together. It should not be a puree but rather a chunky mixture. *Makes 4 cups.*

4 ears fresh corn, cooked, kernels removed
2 avocados, peeled, diced
2 small tomatoes, diced
2 tablespoons minced fresh coriander, or to taste
2 tablespoons lime juice
1 large garlic clove, minced
2 tablespoons minced red onion
2 jalapeño peppers, minced, seeds and ribs removed, or to taste
salt and pepper to taste

ALL-AMERICAN DINNER

MENU

〰 WILD MUSHROOM SALAD

ᔇᔇᔇ BEEF TENDERLOIN WITH JANE'S HORSERADISH SAUCE

❯❯❯ SAUTÉED RED AND YELLOW PEAR TOMATOES

ᨆᨆᨆᨆ BAKED POTATOES

 oooo PEAR CRISP

▪▪▪▪ BEVERAGE: RICH, FULL-BODIED RED WINE

This menu is wonderful to serve either in summer or winter. The horseradish sauce and pear crisp can be made ahead and the beef tenderloin can be assembled, ready for the oven. It is the perfect menu to show off one of your best and favorite red wines.

WILD MUSHROOM SALAD

Separate leaves and wash radicchio. Wrap in paper towels and a plastic bag, then store in refrigerator until ready to use.

Remove and discard stems from mushrooms and slice. Smash garlic clove with flat side of a knife. In a large skillet heat olive oil and garlic, being careful not to burn garlic. Add pine nuts and brown lightly. Add prosciutto and mushrooms. Sauté. When mushrooms begin to soften, add sherry vinegar and boil down to reduce slightly. Add chives, parsley, and salt and pepper. Adjust seasonings to taste.

Arrange radicchio on salad plates and top each serving with some of warm mushroom mixture.

Variation: Serve as an hors d'oeuvre by separating radicchio leaves. Set aside smallest leaves to use. Save remaining leaves for another time. Fill each leaf with some of mushroom mixture and serve at room temperature on a tray.

2–3 heads radicchio
10 ounces assorted fresh wild mushrooms
1 clove garlic
5 tablespoons olive oil
2 tablespoons pine nuts
1½ ounces prosciutto, chopped (optional)
2 tablespoons sherry vinegar
1 tablespoon minced fresh chives
2 tablespoons minced fresh parsley
salt and pepper to taste

ON WILD MUSHROOMS...

Wild mushrooms can be costly to purchase. To cut down on the cost, substitute half of the wild mushrooms called for in a recipe with domestic mushrooms. You will still get enough of the "wild" flavor.

BEEF TENDERLOIN

Preheat oven to 425°.

Rub fillet all over with cut side of garlic. Coat beef with olive oil and press pepper into meat.

Set beef in a shallow roasting pan. Bake for 10 minutes. Reduce heat to 350° and bake for about 20 minutes for rare (120° on thermometer) or 30 minutes for medium (130°). Remove from oven and let stand for 10 minutes before slicing.

2½–3 pounds fillet of beef wrapped in fat
1 clove garlic, halved
¼ cup olive oil
2 tablespoons freshly ground black pepper or a mixture of white, black, and green peppercorns

JANE'S HORSERADISH SAUCE

This recipe comes from my college roommate, Jane Mitchell, and is the perfect simple sauce to dress up the Beef Tenderloin.

1 cup cream cheese,
    softened
1 cup sour cream
1 tablespoon crème fraîche
2–4 tablespoons
    horseradish to taste
lemon juice to taste
salt and pepper to taste
1 teaspoon Dijon mustard

In the bowl of a food processor process cream cheese until smooth. Add remaining ingredients. Adjust seasonings and serve with tenderloin. *Makes 2 cups.*

SAUTÉED RED AND YELLOW PEAR TOMATOES

At certain times of the year you can find red and yellow pear-shaped tomatoes. They have a wonderful flavor and are a nice change from red cherry tomatoes.

2 tablespoons olive oil
1 pint red pear or cherry
    tomatoes, stemmed
    and halved
1 pint yellow pear or
    cherry tomatoes,
    stemmed and
    halved
1 tablespoon fresh herbs
    (your choice)
salt and pepper to taste

In a skillet heat olive oil. Add tomatoes and season with herbs, salt and pepper. Sauté for 3 to 5 minutes, or until tomatoes are slightly softened.

PEAR CRISP

Preheat oven to 350°. Grease a 9″-x-13″ baking dish.

Slice pears crosswise ¼ inch thick. Arrange slices in rows, slightly overlapping, in baking dish.

In a food processor process butter, flour, walnuts, brown sugar, lemon zest, cinnamon, and nutmeg until mixture resembles coarse crumbs. Sprinkle over pears and drizzle bourbon over top.

Bake for 20 minutes, or until brown and crisp. Serve with whipped cream.

6 medium pears, peeled
    and cored
6 tablespoons butter,
    cut into 6 pieces
    and chilled
½ cup flour
½ cup chopped walnuts
6 tablespoons brown
    sugar
grated zest of 1 lemon
½ teaspoon ground
    cinnamon
¼ teaspoon grated
    nutmeg
3 tablespoons bourbon
1 cup heavy cream,
    whipped

ON WHIPPED CREAM...

1. *To whip 1 cup heavy cream several hours in advance and keep it from weeping, add 2 tablespoons confectioners' sugar and 1 tablespoon liqueur when soft peaks start to form.*
2. *Use ice cube trays to freeze leftover whipped cream. When frozen, transfer to freezer bags. After defrosting for 20 minutes, drop cream in your coffee cup for a treat.*

ENTERTAINING THOUGHTS

This menu requires some last-minute cooking, so here are a variety of simple suggestions for no-cook nibbles to serve with drinks before dinner:

Cheese straws

Spiced nuts

Marinated artichoke hearts

Smoked salmon canapés

Ramekins of assorted olives

Variety of sliced salamis

Sliced smoked chicken, turkey, duck, or goose

Wedge of Brie skewered with a red grape

Crackers spread with cream cheese, topped with a pretty cutout of sun-dried tomato

Black bread cut into 1-inch rounds, spread with Boursin cheese, topped with a slice of plum tomato, garnished with a basil leaf

MEXICAN FIESTA NIGHT

MENU

o o o JANICE'S
PRIZEWINNING CHILI

vvvv SALAD BOWL
GARNISH

••••• JALAPEÑO CORN
BREAD

eeeee MINT CHOCOLATE
COOKIE BARS

◢◢◢◢ BEVERAGE:
BEER

I think I can safely say that I now like Mexican cuisine more than French! Mexican fare allows you the freedom to have a casual evening, possibly with everyone helping themselves straight from a pot on the stove. This recipe from Janice Burne has been slightly adapted by me. The original won first runner-up as the Pepsico entry in the International Chili Cookoff contest!

Janice's Prizewinning Chili

Chili can be served on squares of corn bread, in warm taco shells, or in hot-dog rolls. Serve with Salad Bowl Garnish.

In a large pot heat olive oil. Add onions, garlic, and jalapeño peppers. Sauté until softened, about 10 minutes. Remove and set aside.

In same pot crumble sausage meat and ground beef and cook, stirring often, until brown. Drain off fat.

Add onion mixture to meat. Add seasonings, then tomato paste, tomato sauce, and red wine. Bring to the boil. Lower heat and simmer for 15 minutes.

- 2 tablespoons olive oil
- ½ pound onions, coarsely chopped
- 4 cloves garlic, minced
- 2 jalapeño peppers, seeds removed, minced
- ½ pound sweet sausage
- 2 pounds coarsely ground chopped meat
- 3 tablespoons chili powder
- 2 tablespoons ground cumin
- 1 teaspoon salt
- black pepper to taste
- 1 tablespoon dried basil
- 1 tablespoon dried oregano
- 3 ounces tomato paste
- 1½ cups tomato sauce
- ¼ cup red wine

Entertaining Thoughts

Entertaining casually provides so many side benefits. For instance, you can use bandanas for napkins. They look great, are inexpensive to buy, and you can toss them in the washer after dinner. So much easier than fancy-occasion linen or lacy napkins.

Salad Bowl Garnish

In separate small bowls set out these garnishes to serve with the chili.

- shredded lettuce
- minced onions
- sour cream
- grated cheddar cheese
- chopped jalapeño peppers

Jalapeño Corn Bread

1 cup flour
1 cup yellow cornmeal
¼ cup sugar
1¼ teaspoons baking soda
½ teaspoon salt
½ cup sour cream
¾ cup buttermilk or
  plain yogurt
2 eggs
2 tablespoons corn oil
1 jalapeño pepper,
  minced

Preheat oven to 425°. Grease an 8-inch square pan or corn stick molds.

In a large bowl combine dry ingredients. In a separate bowl mix together wet ingredients and jalapeño. Add wet mixture to dry mixture.

Place in pan or molds. Bake for 15 to 18 minutes in the pan, or 7 to 10 minutes in corn stick molds, or until golden brown.

Mint Chocolate Cookie Bars

2 sticks (1 cup) butter,
  softened
1 cup brown sugar
1 egg yolk
1 teaspoon vanilla
  extract
2 cups sifted flour
1½ cups mint chocolate
  chips
1 cup coarsely chopped
  walnuts

Preheat oven to 350°. Grease a 9″-x-13″ baking pan.

In the bowl of an electric mixer cream butter and brown sugar. Add egg yolk and vanilla. Beat well. Add flour and stir to combine.

Spread batter in a thin layer in pan. Bake for 25 minutes. Remove from oven. Spread mint chips evenly on top of batter and bake for 3 minutes more. Remove from oven and, with a knife, spread melted chocolate into an even layer. Sprinkle walnuts evenly on top. Cool in pan before cutting into bars. *Makes 24 bars.*

Simple Fiesta Centerpiece...

One of my mother-in-law's favorite centerpieces is to display a variety of small cactus plants in clay pots. This is the perfect centerpiece for a Mexican Fiesta dinner. You might want to put one at each guest's place for them to take home as party favors.

DINNER FOR A WINTER EVENING

MENU

PORK MEDALLIONS
WITH PRUNES

BABY CARROTS WITH
BALSAMIC VINEGAR

GRATIN OF
POTATOES AND
ONIONS

PORT MELON CUP

BEVERAGE:
RICH, FULL-BODIED
RED WINE

Janice Burne's recipe for Pork Medallions with Prunes is a winning combination and a wonderful wintery dish served with these unusual carrots and a soothing gratin of potatoes and onions. The pork medallions and the carrots may be cooked ahead and gently reheated. Also, scoop out melon balls ahead. Prepare potatoes shortly before serving time.

PORK MEDALLIONS WITH PRUNES

6 tablespoons butter
3 onions, diced
30 pitted prunes, halved
1½ cups apple juice
2¼ pounds pork
    tenderloin, sliced
    into ¼-inch
    medallions
salt and pepper to taste
2 tablespoons oil
½ cup heavy cream

In a skillet melt 4 tablespoons butter. Add onions and sauté for 5 minutes, or until softened. Add prunes. Pour in apple juice and bring to the boil. Reduce heat and simmer for 5 minutes. Pour into bowl and set aside.

Season pork with salt and pepper. In same skillet melt remaining 2 tablespoons butter and oil together. When hot, add pork and sauté for about 10 minutes, or until done, turning once. Remove to serving dish.

Add cream to skillet, raise heat, and scrape up any browned particles. Add prune mixture. When heated through, pour over pork and serve.

BABY CARROTS WITH BALSAMIC VINEGAR

3 12-ounce packages
    baby carrots,
    peeled
6 tablespoons water
8 tablespoons butter
salt to taste
7 tablespoons brown
    sugar
1 tablespoon balsamic
    vinegar

In a saucepan combine carrots, water, 2 tablespoons butter, and salt. Cover and bring to the boil. Lower heat and simmer for 15 minutes, or until tender. Most of the water will be absorbed.

In a small saucepan combine sugar, remaining 6 tablespoons butter, and vinegar. Cook until butter is melted and mixture is well blended. Pour over carrots and serve.

N O T E : *Carrots can be cooked ahead, but left slightly underdone, and sauce also can be prepared ahead of time. Reheat sauce with carrots when ready to serve.*

GRATIN OF POTATOES AND ONIONS

Preheat oven to 375°. Grease a 14-inch gratin dish.

In a saucepan combine cream, milk, salt, pepper, and nutmeg. Heat until warm. Arrange potatoes and onions in alternating layers in gratin dish. Dot top with butter. Pour cream mixture over top and bake for 40 to 50 minutes.

1 cup heavy cream
1½ cups milk
1 teaspoon salt
black pepper to taste
pinch grated nutmeg
1 pound boiling
    potatoes, peeled,
    thinly sliced
1 pound onions, thinly
    sliced
3 tablespoons butter

PORT MELON CUP

At a wonderful little restaurant in upstate New York, this was served to clear the palate between courses. It was a terrific idea but, better yet, it is a wonderful quick dessert that includes an afterdinner liqueur at the same time!

Using a tiny melon baller scoop out 24 melon balls. Place 4 balls in the bottom of a liqueur glass. Fill glass with Port and serve with biscotti.

cantaloupe
Port
biscotti

ENTERTAINING THOUGHTS

Start a "dinner party book." I started one at least ten years ago. In it I record the date of the event, who I invited, what the occasion was, the seating arrangement, the menu, wine served, and any special comments. For example, I now know not to serve eggplant when one friend is invited to dinner because his first course went back to the kitchen untouched!

*O*N WINTER FOODS...

Winter is the time we think of roaring fires, wild game, Christmas, and all sorts of citrus fruits as well. Here are foods that are plentiful in the markets when the weather turns cold:

Tangelos
Clementines
Blood oranges
Star ruby grapefruit
Jaffa oranges
Plantains

Fennel
Parsnips
Wild game
Fruit cakes
Hot spiced cider

FANCY TAKE-OUT

GOURMET TO GO

MENU

HOT-AND-SOUR SOUP 〰〰〰

ASSORTED DIM SUM WITH DIPPING SAUCES 〰

STIR-FRIED VEGETABLES ○ ○ ○

RICE ,,,,

FORTUNE COOKIES ·····

PASTRIES ○○○○

BEVERAGE: CHINESE TEA ʌ ʌ ʌ

Entertaining in the eighties means cooking smart. Maybe it even means not cooking at all! There are all kinds of foods available by take-out, so take your pick.

This menu is based on an assortment of dim sum that will give you an all-appetizer dinner. Composed of many small delicacies, dim sum is difficult to cook at home, but easy to carry out. Call your favorite Chinese restaurant and ask for suggestions of available varieties. Round out the meal with hot-and-sour soup for a starter and some stir-fried vegetables (see Vegetable Stir-Fry, page 99 if you want to make your own) and rice to accompany the dim sum. You can pick up everything including chopsticks, fortune cookies, and even Chinese tea bags. For extra freshness, you can steam the dumplings yourself at home. Ask your restaurant for heating instructions. As a general rule, 10 to 12 minutes steaming time is sufficient, except for pork items, which take 20 minutes. Because you are not doing the cooking, you can devote your time to creating a Chinese teahouse atmosphere. Appropriate touches would be bamboo place mats and chopsticks. Use a lazy Susan for the dipping sauces, and bamboo steamer baskets and trays for serving. For a fun finale, read your fortunes around the table!

MAIN COURSE TAKE-OUT...

Take-out is the low-key approach when you want to supplement your own efforts and not hire a caterer. You can purchase either hors d'oeuvres, main courses, go-withs, or desserts and cook the rest of the menu yourself. For instance, you can greatly enhance main course take-out ribs by preparing first course crabcakes, biscuits, and a fruit pie. Make sure to sample ahead of time and adjust flavors to your own taste.

Here are some suggestions for take-out main courses:

Lasagna	*Veal or lamb stew*
Chili	*Manicotti*
Roast chicken	*Fillet of beef*
Spare ribs	*Chicken potpies*
Poached salmon	*Cooked shrimp*

COME FOR COCKTAILS AND ANTIPASTO

*E*very time you have company, keep in mind that you don't always have to serve dinner. For instance, this is a perfect way to entertain when you invite friends to watch the Super Bowl. You prepare 2 of the dishes and supplement with the best available from your local Italian deli. Set everything out, beautifully arranged, in wonderful baskets. Display the olives in assorted crocks, each labeled with the appropriate name tag.

MENU

BAKED STUFFED ARTICHOKE HEARTS

RED-TONGUED BOCCONCHINI

ASSORTED SALAMIS

ROASTED RED PEPPERS

OLIVE TASTING

BAKED GARLIC

VARIETY OF BREADS

BEVERAGE: LIGHT, FRUITY RED WINE

Baked Stuffed Artichoke Hearts

2 14-ounce cans
    artichoke hearts
1 cup bread crumbs
¼ cup toasted pine nuts
5 tablespoons grated
    Parmesan cheese
2 tablespoons olive oil

Preheat oven to 350°.

Drain artichoke hearts and arrange on baking sheet. Cut in half if artichokes are too large. In the bowl of a food processor fitted with a steel blade combine bread crumbs, pine nuts, 4 tablespoons Parmesan, and olive oil. Spoon some of bread crumb mixture on top of each heart. Sprinkle with remaining tablespoon Parmesan and drizzle additional olive oil on top. Bake for 10 minutes, or until browned. *Makes 24.*

Red-Tongued Bocconchini

1 pound mozzarella
    cheese
sun-dried tomatoes
¼ cup extra-virgin olive
    oil
dried crushed hot red
    pepper flakes to taste
2 tablespoons chopped
    fresh basil
black pepper to taste
curly lettuce leaves

Using a melon baller, cut out mozzarella into bocconchini bites (1- to 2-inch balls). Slice crosswise, not cutting all the way through. Insert a piece of sun-dried tomato between the 2 halves, leaving a little "tongue" protruding.

In a shallow dish combine olive oil, crushed red pepper flakes, basil, and black pepper. Add bocconchini and carefully roll around to coat with oil mixture. Thread each bite on a long bamboo skewer. Serve on a bed of curly lettuce.

On Skewers...

Long bamboo skewers are much prettier to use than little toothpicks when an item needs to be skewered. Just remember to have something nearby in which to dispose of the skewers. A glass vase is perfect. Place one used skewer in the vase so guests know what it's for. There's nothing worse than walking around during the cocktail hour holding used skewers!

Baked Garlic

This recipe takes 5 minutes to assemble and an hour to cook, but since it doesn't need any watching I decided it was worth including.

Preheat oven to 300°.

Break apart cloves of garlic but leave skin on. Arrange in a small baking dish and cover with olive oil. Sprinkle on thyme, salt, and pepper. Bake for 1 hour, or until garlic is soft.

Squeeze garlic out of skin and into a small bowl. Mash together with butter and some of the olive oil. Serve in a crock with warm Italian bread.

1 head of garlic
½ cup olive oil
2 sprigs fresh thyme, or
    ½ teaspoon dried
salt and pepper to taste
4 tablespoons butter,
    softened
1 loaf Italian bread

Entertaining Thoughts

One of the best ways to save time in the kitchen is in the hors d'oeuvre area. Fortunately, there is a wide variety available through take-out. Be sure to taste test first and make any necessary adjustments to flavors. If you are creative enough, just about anything can be taken out—all you have to do is ask!

Here are some take-out suggestions:

Egg rolls

Assorted dim sum

Sushi

Sashimi platter

Antipasto tray

"Gourmet" pizzas you cut into squares

Cooked shrimp and cocktail sauce

Oysters on the half shell

Stuffed grape leaves

Spanikopita (spinach pie)

*Frozen pastry-type hors
    d'oeuvres*

Barbecued baby ribs

*Fish spreads (caviar, smoked
    salmon, smoked tuna)*

Hummus

Quiche

Brie baked in pastry

SALADS ALL AROUND

MENU

//// TORTELLINI SALAD

^ ^ ^ PÂTÉS

o o o VARIETY OF SALAMIS
AND MUSTARDS

//// CROCKS OF OLIVES

▪▪▪▪▪ MARINATED
VEGETABLES

ﻮﻮﻮ ITALIAN CHEESES

~~~ ASSORTED BREADS

ⵯⵯⵯ ITALIAN ICES OR
ICED ESPRESSO
(OPTIONAL)

ℓℓℓℓℓ BEVERAGE:
BLOODY MARYS

A great time to entertain is on Sunday, whether it's for lunch or an early dinner. This rather extensive menu has only one recipe that you prepare yourself. The rest is all in the display. Go to the best Italian deli to shop for the remaining foodstuffs.

The larger the variety the more interesting the buffet. Serve a variety of salamis, mustards, and olives. It might be a good idea to label the items so guests know what they're eating! Some excellent choices for olives are Kalamata, Greek, Niçoise, Sicilian, and Gaeta. The salad recipe is for 6 but *can be doubled, depending on the number of guests. If you want to serve dessert, serve Italian ices or iced espresso.*

TORTELLINI SALAD

Bring a large pot of salted water to the boil.

In a bowl beat together vinegar, Dijon, salt and pepper. Slowly whisk in olive oil in a thin stream. Stir in parsley and basil. Set aside.

Cook tortellini according to package directions. Drain in a colander. Toss with dressing to coat and set aside to cool slightly. Add peppers, green onions, cheese, and nuts. Serve at room temperature.

Variation: Tortellini can also be served slightly drained of dressing on long skewers as an hors d'oeuvre, omitting red and yellow peppers.

DRESSING:

¼ cup red wine vinegar
1½ teaspoons Dijon mustard
salt and pepper to taste
1 cup olive oil
2 tablespoons minced fresh parsley
3 tablespoons minced fresh basil

1½ pounds cheese-filled spinach tortellini
¼ cup julienned red bell peppers
¼ cup julienned yellow bell peppers
⅓ cup thinly sliced green onions
2 tablespoons grated Parmesan cheese
¼ cup toasted pine nuts

OTHER TAKE-OUT POSSIBILITIES...

Japanese Restaurants—*platters of sushi and sashimi*
Italian Delis—*antipasto salads, six-foot hero sandwiches, trays of lasagne and manicotti, fresh pasta, sauces you can enhance with fresh herbs, and pizza dough for baking your own pie*
Fish Markets—*cooked shrimp and cocktail sauce, cooked lobsters, cold poached salmon and dill sauce, oysters and clams on the half shell, assorted smoked fish (tuna, eel, bluefish, salmon) with your own curried mayonnaise dip*
Greek Restaurants—*stuffed grape leaves, Greek salad, and spinach pie*
Gourmet Shops—*chili (you add the fixings), whole roast chicken, frozen pastry-type hors d'oeuvres, whole glazed ham, chocolate mousse, fruit pies and cheesecake for dessert*
Bakeries—*great breads (for deli fare), croissants (for sandwiches or a breakfast buffet), cakes and assorted cookies*

PASTA

Company Pasta Dinner

MENU

ITALIAN SALAD

ANGEL HAIR PASTA WITH SHRIMP SAUCE

BROCCOLI WITH OIL AND GARLIC

WHOLE-WHEAT FRENCH BREAD

ELLEN'S TIPSY BAKED PEACHES

BEVERAGE: DRY, MEDIUM-BODIED WHITE WINE

*W*hen this recipe for angel hair pasta first appeared in New Woman *magazine as a Short Order for Everyday recipe, Donna Jackson, a senior editor, said it was so good she served it for company. So it is one of the many recipes that can make the transition from an "everyday" to a "company" main course.*

The salad dressing and broccoli can be prepared ahead of time. The pasta dish needs to be prepared just before serving. The peaches can be assembled in advance and put in the oven just before sitting down to dinner.

ITALIAN SALAD

In a bowl whisk together vinegar, salt, and pepper. Slowly drizzle in olive oil, while continuing to whisk. Stir in onions and set aside for at least 1 hour before serving.

To serve, toss lettuce together with vinaigrette and crumble blue cheese on top.

VINAIGRETTE:

¼ cup red wine vinegar
salt and pepper to taste
½ cup olive oil
1 yellow onion, thinly
   sliced

1–2 heads of Boston
   lettuce, leaves
   separated
1 bunch arugula, stems
   removed
2 ounces blue cheese,
   crumbled

ANGEL HAIR PASTA WITH SHRIMP SAUCE

Bring large pot of salted water to the boil. In a saucepan combine heavy cream and shallots. Bring to the boil for 10 minutes, or until cream reduces and thickens slightly. Add shrimp and cook for 3 minutes more. Stir in pepper, nutmeg, and basil.

Cook pasta in boiling salted water according to package directions. Drain. Arrange pasta in a large bowl, make a well in center for sauce and toss at the table.

4 cups heavy cream
3 shallots, finely chopped
1 pound shrimp,
   deveined and cut
   into bite-size pieces
¼ teaspoon black pepper
¼ teaspoon grated
   nutmeg
¼ cup chpped fresh basil
1½ pounds angel hair
   pasta or any very
   thin pasta noodle

BROCCOLI WITH OIL AND GARLIC

In a skillet gently heat olive oil, garlic, and pepper flakes. Turn up heat and add broccoli. Cover and cook for 5 minutes, or until tender. Serve hot or at room temperature.

3 tablespoons olive oil
1 clove garlic, crushed
1 teaspoon crushed red
   pepper flakes
2 bunches broccoli,
   stems separated

ELLEN'S TIPSY BAKED PEACHES

These peaches can be assembled ahead of time and put in the oven when you sit down to dinner. They are ready to serve when you are.

1 pound can peach halves, with their syrup
1 tablespoon brown sugar
2 tablespoons maple syrup
½ teaspoon ground cinnamon
¼ cup brandy, warmed
1 quart vanilla ice cream

Preheat oven to 350°. Grease a baking dish.

Arrange peaches, along with syrup, cut side up in the baking dish. Sprinkle on brown sugar, maple syrup, and cinnamon. Bake for 30 to 45 minutes. Remove from oven.

Pour brandy over peaches, and ignite at the table, being careful to avert your face. Serve warm peaches and sauce over vanilla ice cream.

Variation: Peaches can be served with sauce and garnished with whipped cream.

ON PASTA...

1. *To measure uncooked dried spaghetti, place a quarter on a piece of paper and draw a circle on it. Grab a handful of pasta and stand it upright on the circle. The amount that completely covers the circle is about 4 ounces—enough for 1 serving.*

2. *Thin spaghetti is best for seafood sauces and any sauce with an olive oil base. Regular spaghetti is good for butter-based sauces and tomato sauces. Use substantial pasta, like rigatoni, with meat sauces.*

3. *Pasta presented unmixed looks prettier, so arrange pasta in a bowl and spoon sauce on top in the center without tossing together. This also keeps the pasta from getting soggy.*

ON SHRIMP...

Fresh jumbo shrimp are more costly than smaller ones. If you aren't planning on serving them whole, buy the smaller ones. However, they will take longer to shell and devein, so consider asking the fishmonger to do that for you.

MENU

PASTA WITH FRESH
UNCOOKED
TOMATO SAUCE

CAESAR SALAD

BREADSTICKS

WINE BISCUITS

ESPRESSO WITH
SAMBUCA

BEVERAGE:
LIGHT, FRUITY
RED WINE

During the summer months, when tomatoes and fresh basil are crowding the markets, farmstands, and possibly even your own backyard, this pasta dish is the perfect main course. This recipe couldn't be easier or more inexpensive to make during the late summer. The sauce can be made earlier in the day, if you like. And so can the salad up to a point. Serve wine biscuits with the espresso at meal's end. (These are available at gourmet shops or Italian groceries.)

PASTA WITH FRESH UNCOOKED TOMATO SAUCE

1½ pounds ripe
    tomatoes
¾ cup olive oil
½ cup coarsely chopped
    fresh basil
2½ teaspoons dried
    oregano
salt and pepper to taste
6 tablespoons halved,
    pitted black olives
6 tablespoons grated
    Parmesan cheese
1½ pounds pasta
    (spaghetti or linguini)
12 ounces mozzarella
    cheese, cubed

Remove core from tomatoes, cut in half, and gently squeeze out the seeds. Cube tomatoes and put in glass bowl with olive oil. Add basil, oregano, salt and pepper, and toss to combine. Add olives and Parmesan. Refrigerate until ready to serve. (This may be made in the morning, if desired.)

Bring a large pot of salted water to the boil. Cook pasta according to package directions. Drain in a colander and place on a serving dish. Top with cubed mozzarella and tomato sauce. Toss and serve at the table.

CAESAR SALAD

My husband and I love Caesar salad but he hates it when an egg is tossed in (as do many people). This recipe eliminates the egg, and, I think, tastes just as good—if not better!

1 tin flat anchovies,
    chopped
2 cloves garlic, smashed
½ cup olive oil
1 head of romaine
    lettuce, torn
¾ teaspoon
    Worcestershire sauce
juice of ½ lemon
1 cup grated Parmesan
    cheese
freshly ground black pepper to taste
croutons

In a bowl combine anchovies, garlic, and olive oil. Set aside. (Make in the morning if possible and leave at room temperature to "marinate.") Remove garlic cloves before using.

Arrange torn lettuce in a salad bowl. Toss with olive oil mixture, Worcestershire, and lemon juice. Add Parmesan and pepper. Toss well and add croutons before serving.

ESPRESSO WITH SAMBUCA

Prepare espresso with your favorite ground beans or use instant powdered espresso. Bring a bottle of Sambuca to the table and add a splash to each cup.

ON COOKING PASTA...

1. *To cut down on time, cover the pot when bringing a large amount of water to the boil.*
2. *Use at least 4 quarts water to cook up to 1 pound pasta. After the water comes to a boil, add 1½ tablespoons salt.*
3. *Add a small amount of olive oil to the boiling water to prevent the strands of pasta from sticking together.*
4. *When cooking long strands of pasta, don't break them to fit the pot. Ease them into the water as they become soft.*
5. *Fresh pasta only needs to cook for 1 to 2 minutes, depending on the thickness of the strands.*
6. *It is not necessary to rinse pasta under cold water after it is cooked.*
7. *When making a cold pasta salad, toss the pasta with a little olive oil immediately after cooking to prevent the strands from sticking together.*

A QUICK CENTERPIECE...

Use apples as candleholders. Remove the core and a thin slice from the bottom of the apple so it will stand upright. Insert a candle in the hollow core and surround with Galax leaves or snippets of boxwood.

APPENDIX

THE MAIL ORDER WAY

Mail order is becoming a great boon to the person with limited time. Also, it is quite helpful for the person who doesn't live near a big city with numerous gourmet shops. There is quite a wide array of items available. The only tricky thing is that for some perishable foods you need to be there to accept delivery so they can be refrigerated. You might want to consider having delivery made to your office.

So, pick up your telephone or pencil and paper and start ordering. The following is a helpful list to get you started.

Alaska Wild Berry Products
528 East Pioneer Avenue
Homer, AK 99603
(907) 235-8858

American Spoon Foods
411 East Lake Street
Petoskey, MI 49770
(616) 347-9030

Arnold Reuben Jr.'s
Cheesecakes
15 Hillpark Avenue
Great Neck, NY 11021
(516) 466-3685

Balducci's
424 Avenue of the Americas
New York, NY 10011
(800) 431-9003; (212) 673-2600

Caviarteria Inc.
29 East 60th Street
New York, NY 10022
(800) 221-1021; (212) 759-7410

The Clambake Co.
P.O. Box 1677
Orleans, MA 02653
(617) 255-3289

Club du Faison
P.O. Box 155
Sugar Loaf, NY 10981
(914) 469-9902

Community Coffee Co.
P.O. Box 3778
Baton Rouge, LA 70821
(800) 535-9901

Dean & Deluca
Mail Order Dept.
110 Greene Street, Suite 304
New York, NY 10012
(800) 221-7714

Deborah's Country French
Bread
500 North Orleans
Chicago, IL 60610
(800) 952-1400; (312) 321-6021

Desserts by David Glass
140–150 Huyshope Avenue
Hartford, CT 06106
(203) 525-0345

The Ethnic Pantry
P.O. Box 798
Grayslake, IL 60030
(312) 223-6660

Glie Farms
1600 Bathgate Avenue
Bronx, NY 10457
(212) 731-2130

Grace Tea Company
80 Fifth Avenue
New York, NY 10011
(212) 255-2935

Harrington's in Vermont
670 B-5 Main Street
Richmond, VT 05477
(802) 434-4444

Hay Day
Mail Order Dept.
907 Post Road East
Westport, CT 06880
(203) 227-9008

Katagiri
224 East 59th Street
New York, NY 10022
(212) 755-3566

Oakville Grocery
7856 St. Helena Highway
P.O. Box 86
Oakville, CA 94562
(707) 944-8802

Omaha Steaks International
P.O. Box 3300
Omaha, NE 68103
(800) 228-2778

Pamela Krausmann's Notebooks
496 LaGuardia Place
Dept. 193
New York, NY 10012
(212) 473-8002

The Silver Palate
274 Columbus Avenue
New York, NY 10023
(212) 799-6340

Simply Shortbread
1314 Ocean Avenue
San Francisco, CA 94112
(415) 333-2400

Vanns Spices
P.O. Box 582
Brooklandville, MD 21022
(301) 583-1643

Williams-Sonoma
Mail Order Dept.
P.O. Box 7456
San Francisco, CA 94120-7456

Zabar's
249 West 80th Street
New York, NY 10024
(212) 787-2002

WINE

The menus in this book suggest wines by several different categories. The following is a list of my personal favorites, which may give you an idea of what to select.

WHITE WINES

Dry, Light-Bodied:	Dry, Medium-Bodied:	Full-Bodied, Complex Flavor:
Chardonnay	Fumé Blanc	Chablis
Frascati	Gavi	Chardonnay (Oaky)
Gros Plant	Graves	Chassagne-Montrachet
Mâcon-Villages	Mâcon	Corton-Charlemagne
Muscadet	Pouilly-Fuissé	Greco di Tufo
Orvieto	Pouilly-Fumé	Meursault
Pinot Grigio	Saint-Véran	Puligny-Montrachet
Soave	Sancerre	

ROSÉ

Cabernet d'Anjou
Tavel
Vin Gris

RED WINES

Light, Fruity:	Rich, Full-Bodied:	Robust, Very Full-Bodied:
Bardolino	Barbaresco	Barolo
Beaujolais	Bordeaux	Chambertin
Brouilly	Merlot	Châteauneuf-du-Pape
Chianti	Nuits-St.-Georges	Gigondas
Chiroubles	Cabernet Sauvignon	La Tâche
Côtes-du-Rhône	Echézeaux	Zinfandel
Lambrusco	Rioja Reserva	
Valpolicella	Syrah	

INDEX